101
MEN

AND STILL ALONE

101
MEN

AND STILL ALONE

MARILYN MARSH

BALBOA.
PRESS

A DIVISION OF HAY HOUSE

Balboa Press books may be ordered through booksellers or by contacting:

Balboa Press
A Division of Hay House
1663 Liberty Drive
Bloomington, IN 47403
www.balboapress.com
1-(877) 407-4847

Printed in the United States of America

ISBN: 978-1-4525-6750-1 (sc)
ISBN: 978-1-4525-6752-5 (hc)
ISBN: 978-1-4525-6751-8 (e)

Library of Congress Control Number: 2013901434

Balboa Press rev. date: 06/19/2013

INTRODUCTION

What led me to think life was built on sex? My quest to feel that I could be someone for myself and with a partner. I let so many men touch me, play with me, and fuck me, thinking they cared.

I never spent more than a year and a half with any one man (except my first husband). This was "by choice." If I did not feel respected by whatever man I was with or if I felt I was only a body to him and didn't matter to him, I would make plans to leave.

My journey was a process of learning through each man I was with. I read self-help books, sought counseling, and listened to great speakers at venues like John Gray seminars. Louise Hay's books and CDs, Gary Zukav, and so many other great speakers and books helped me along my journey to heal my soul and find my heart.

Why so many men? What lessons was I to learn?

Was it fear of commitment that kept me from being with one partner?

When did I shut down? When did I stop feeling?

Most of us women (and, yes, men too) are not taught at home while we are young about what it means to have a respectful, healthy, loving relationship; nor are we taught how to love ourselves or others.

So life begins, and we are each on our own journey to figure out these lessons. We must learn how to respect ourselves and how to raise kids. The latter is a tough one.

No, I did not have the tools to do this. I was always trying to figure myself out. I was lost in life with no structure. What a mess I was. And being very naive, I did the best I could with the tools I had.

My life's journey began, and I moved from one man to the next. Why so many? The more sex I had, the more I felt inside. Without sex, I felt empty.

PORTLAND MEN EXPOSED

I'm sorry, girlfriends or wives, if the men who appear in this book belonged to you. I did not know.

I am addressing women because I do not think that men will be reading this book. If they do, great.

This book is about sex and, yes, lots of it. You knew that from the title, of course! And just to let you in on a secret, it was more like 201 men of all sizes and shapes. Some of them will turn you on, and some of them will make you want them to put their dicks back in their pants. This book smells of come and is filled with different ways of having sex.

Since I bashed men, I must say that my mom could have taught me to say no or how to feel. Those are big lessons in life. I guess she wasn't shown or taught herself, so of course, she did not know to teach me. And this is the case for many of us out there.

Sorry, men. I do think parents should teach their sons at an early age to respect and like themselves so that they can grow up to be men who like and respect the women in their lives. That is a hard one, since men have two heads and forget which one to think with. And so my story begins.

CHAPTER ONE

MY EARLY YEARS GROWING UP

W E ALL HAVE OUR CHILDHOOD MEMORIES, which direct us as we grow into adults. My memories are few. I recall no hugs or closeness, only empty days; arguing; and noisy, sleepless nights. My dad was an alcoholic. When drinking, he would beat my mom. One night when I was twelve years old, I jumped in to help my mom, and I was getting beat up too, so I ran outside to hide. My dad came looking for me. I hid in the dark. I was scared. Later that night, I crawled through the basement window. I could hear my mom and dad still arguing. My dad was such a nice, loving man when he did not drink. He made sure we had a house. (I say *house* rather than *home* because a home is love and warmth. A house is heat and food.) My mom was a simple woman who left home when she was thirteen. She wasn't educated, and she was a nice woman, though naive.

When I graduated from eighth grade in 1962, I matured into a girl who looked like an eighteen-year-old. I got looks and a lot of attention, and I was asked out by older guys. I had a great body but did not know it at the time. My boobs were a thirty-six, so it seemed.

I started to become aware of my sexuality in the third grade. I experienced feelings as a child that I did not fully understand until later on in life. I seemed to be focused on this feeling related to our sexual parts that no one talked about. I just wanted to do things to myself to keep that feeling, that sensation. I didn't know what was happening or what my body was experiencing, and I had no one to talk to about what was going on.

I taught myself to swim at Blue Lake Park. I went swimming there a lot. Once I cut my foot, and the guy in the park's medical aid office could not get over my feet. He said that I had the most beautiful feet he had ever seen. I would have guys wanting to meet me and coming up to talk to me, but I was shy.

One time I was in the water talking to a boy, and he reached down in the water and touched me inappropriately. When things like that happened, I would just stand there. I did not know how to say *no*. Later, my dad and mom came to pick up me, my sister, and my brother. I asked if I could ride with the boy. I said that I would be okay, that his parents could take me home. I didn't know what to feel; I just knew I was receiving attention. My mind was blank. When I got in their car, the boy who had put his hand on me in the water sat with me in the backseat and did the same thing again. I did not think about whether this was right or wrong. I just blanked out my mind and shut down. This is how it was.

Later, I would learn why I had so many men—sometimes three men a week—and thought the same of each one. After sex, my partner of the moment and I would just lie there and talk as if we were friends. None of the men stood out from the others.

When I had sex, I would always feel it all over my body, every inch. I would think, *Wow, I am alive!* But as soon as we were done, I was empty. My chest felt as if it was made of concrete. I never felt anything from my neck to my waist. I only felt things sexually. I never thought about whether this was normal or right.

HAROLD: THE OLDER MAN

When I was fourteen or maybe fifteen, I met Harold, who was twenty years old. We started dating, and he had a car. My folks were not happy about it, but they let me date him because they trusted me. Little did I know at the time what that really meant.

Harold and I would go to parties where the kids were eighteen to twenty years old. They did not know that I was only fourteen. Afterward, on the way home, we always had sex in the backseat of his car. I just did it thinking that it was the natural thing to do. And, of course, through having sex with him, I would get to feel things in my body. Later this became the only way I knew how to feel.

I did dress to look older than I was; I dressed nicely but with a style that was older than that of other girls my age.

CHAPTER TWO

MARRIED AT A YOUNG AGE

STAN NUMBER ONE AND FIRST HUSBAND, 1963–1974

THEN I MET STAN. THIS was a man who got out of the army and loved once and only once. Born in Oklahoma an Oaky, he had old-fashioned values. He had traveled with the service, so he just wanted to be married and have a home. He did not think that marrying a sixteen-year-old who had not done anything or been anywhere was a problem. My girlfriend's mom and friends were going to Springer's, a dance hall in Gresham. If you were under eighteen, you could go with adults or parents. It was so much fun. I was watching a guy who was very good-looking. He got up on the stage and started singing. He had a dark complexion and coal black hair, and he was tall and slender in his white shirt. I definitely had to meet him. I did, and we made plans to get together. He was on leave from the army. We started dating and, yes, having sex.

He was so good at sex, knowing a woman's body, and it felt good. Stan was the one who taught me how to have great sex. Now I became even more addicted. His cock was crooked, but he knew what he was doing. I started having orgasms with a man. Oh, my God! Once I'd tasted that, it started something inside me in, well in the cunt area. I just needed sex the way some people have to have something to eat.

The song "Soldier Boy" came out, and I bought the record and played it a lot. Stan was too old, my father said. That did not stop me. I was graduating from eighth grade and would become a high school freshman. We had a graduation dance. Stan would not go, so I did not go—darn.

We had sex everywhere—in the car, even while I was babysitting. Sex was my way of feeling something. I said, "I love you," not knowing the meaning or feeling of love or what it meant to be in love. I had no clue about the difference between sex and love.

We talked about getting married. I wanted to go to modeling school and did not want anything to stop me. He said that I could continue with those plans if that was what I wanted. My folks said no, so we planned to go to Utah to get married. He was to pick me up in the middle of the night. The first time we'd scheduled our elopement, I looked out the window and could not do it, so we planned again.

I ran away from home to get married at fifteen years of age. When we got to Utah, we rented an apartment. I called my mom and told her that I was okay.

No one would marry us. After we'd been gone for a month, we decided to go back home. The juvenile authorities were waiting for us. They took me to the juvenile home and Stan to jail. My folks did not file charges, and I was let out to go home. My folks said that we could get married, and we did a month after I turned sixteen, on March 17, 1963.

We bought a trailer to live in. I kept on going to high school. I got pregnant and had my daughter a month after I turned seventeen. As I got older, I started to realize that I was literally doing nothing. I mentioned to Stan that I needed to go to the movies or out to dinner, like on dates. I explained that I needed to get out and enjoy things. He had already traveled with the army and had no interest in going out. I told him that, if he did not take me out by the end of the year, I would leave him. I tried to convince him by suggesting that, if he would take me to a movie or dancing, I would go hunting with him, and we could enjoy with each other the things we both enjoyed. He refused, so at the end of the year, I left him. He was so hurt and shocked.

I went to a dance bar called Division St. Corral. The next thing I knew, I got a call informing me that my husband had been taken to jail. Stan had gotten drunk and tried to enter the dance bar, but the doorman wouldn't let him in. He'd gotten in a fight with the security guards. He wanted his wife. I bailed him out. He was forcefully beaten as a result of his altercation with the Gresham Police. One guy against five officers—that's how our system works.

I went back to him. But I was still asking him to take me out. I wanted us to go and do the normal things that people do. And he was still refusing. In addition, Stan would beat me if I said anything that he did not like. I, of course, knew all the words that he did not like and would say them, knowing what would happen. He would make me sleep on the floor. He treated me very badly. I know now that there are no excuses for his behavior.

Once, I was lying on the floor trying to go to sleep, and I asked him if we could get our bedroom back with the full bed that my mother-in-law was using. He got up and started hitting me again, and I did not feel anything.

But then, he was yelling, "Oh, my God, what did I do?" So I started yelling a lot too. I guess one entire side of my face was so swollen that he took me to the emergency room at the hospital.

I got pregnant again. I planned this pregnancy. I gave birth to a son in 1969, my favorite number. I loved that position.

My mom played Bunco. One day, the game was going to be at her house, and she asked if I would sit in. I said yes. Stan took me and fought with me all the way. I was just going to be at my mom's, but he did not approve. It was another big fight.

We went on vacation to Santiago with his sister, and I wanted to see a few sights—the wax museum, things like that. We did nothing, just walking around sightseeing. We did not go into any place of interest.

When I turned twenty-one, I wanted to go dancing and have a drink in a real bar. Stan took me with some neighbor friends of ours. He would not dance with me, but he allowed me to have one drink and dinner. I felt controlled and confined, unable to do anything, as if I were locked or chained in a room. I had felt this way throughout my life for as long as I could remember—that every man I dated would put me in a locked room and that I could not live my own life. So it was hard to let go of my fear of being confined for years.

I sought psychological help through a number of avenues—books, counseling, seminars, everything that I could think of to break this feeling. Doing so took over ten years.

It was hard for me to compromise with Stan when he could not compromise. Basically it was his way or nothing. I would discover years later that this was the type of man I would continue to attract—men who insisted on their way or nothing. But I was maturing at the time and wanted more. I believed that I was a good mom, and I loved my kids. I had to get a divorce. I was twenty-two years old. We had a big fight over the kids. He put me down in court, but, as it went, he lost. He was so sick over losing his family that he got an ulcer and went to the hospital. But he would not let me see him.

When he was released, I told him that he could stay at my home so that he could be close to his kids. He shared a room with my son. Our living situation worked out fine.

———⦿———

When I was free and divorced, I went wild. I partied hard, making up for the years I'd missed as a teenager and young woman. I went crazy; I thought I had to be out every night. I was sure that I must have missed something out there.

In the bars, I danced, moved, and dressed sexy. I thought that was what a woman did—that she always looked sexy. And I would get noticed. I was different than most girls. I didn't understand why some women dressed plain. In addition, I worked hard. I had years to make up for all the things I'd missed out on. I went out all the time.

And I had sex with the good-looking guys in the bands. They liked me, right? I would meet guys and have sex. Being very naive, I thought that, because they wanted to get in my pants, they must have liked me. This was more than sex, right? Who was I kidding? I realize that now years later.

My sister said that I was meeting so many men when we would go out because of my long hair that fell to my waist like Delilah's. She said that, if I cut it off, I would not get any attention. I did not think she was right. At one time, I had short hair, and I learned that what she said wasn't true. I still had the attention. I just have a look.

What was I looking for? I didn't know. I'd never realistically contemplated that question. I just knew that every time I was about to get exclusive with a guy, I would get sick or would feel like I was going to end up being locked in a room like—chained up and never allowed to get out.

I know my reaction to commitment was tied to my ex keeping me from going anywhere. I found commitment was something that took years to understand. I felt everyone would be the same as my husband—that I'd end up locked in a room and never able to do anything or go anywhere.

When Stan and I were together, we'd just do things at home or with family. Getting over the results of Stan's confinement of me took many years.

Stan and I would work with the kids together later in the years. If he had a date, he would want me to meet the woman and to get my approval. Odd, but yes he did. Or he'd want me to take the woman he was dating with me to the river or the movies because going out, as we know, is not what he does. Stan had tried to take me on a date several times, and he'd always gotten sick. It just wasn't him.

Years later, Stan got sick with Huntington's disease. I made sure he was taken care of at his care home, or I would move him to the next. I was an overseer for him. My kids were busy with three kids each, and I had time. If the nursing home or care home did not do right by him, I would move him. No matter how he treated me in the early years, he was the kids' dad, and I just had to make sure he was taken care of. I would visit him once a month and take him candy bars or things he might need or take him to buy shoes.

He did not want his brothers or sisters to see him that way. He would only let his nephew, who had Huntington's, also visit; they were close.

One time, Stan had fallen at the care home he was staying in, and the facilitators did not call my daughter until the next morning. It seemed the home facilitators did not have a heart; the residents were just bodies to most of them. We all went up to OHU to see him. He was not doing well, and the doctors gave him a few days to live. It was a few weeks before he passed away.

Kenny, Stan's nephew who had Huntington's, came up to see him. Kenny was a special man with a great wife and daughter. He was not doing well with his Huntington's, and after seeing Stan in the hospital, he went home and talked to his wife about not wanting her to go through this with him; he was going to go through the same stages that he'd watched Stan go through. No doctor would give him a pill that would help him die. He had a talk with his wife and daughter and told them he was going to kill himself; he wanted their permission. He explained that he felt that this was what he needed to do so they would not be burdened by his illness.

They said they understood, and one morning, Kenny's wife got up and found that Kenny had shot himself in the bathtub. He wanted to go with Stan, as Stan's passing was going to be any day.

Stan passed away a few days later. We had a funeral for both of them together, as that's how they wanted it. As I am writing, I am crying. Losing Kenny was so sad, and Stan was in a much better place after years of living with the debilitating disease.

I know I loved Stan and worried about him and cared for him. As for being *in* love, I don't know; I did not know back when we were together what it meant to be in love. For years, I would dream that we were in the same bed together. The kids would be with us, and we'd all be laughing together as a family. I would dream I was trying to find him and my family. Everyone, including our family and friends, was shocked that we'd parted in the first place. No one knows what is going on inside another's home.

CHAPTER THREE

EXPERIENCING DATING

STEVE: THE DENTIST

I HAD A DENTIST APPOINTMENT, AND there he was. Steve, my dentist, was so good-looking. He was wholesome and a very nice guy. We decided to get together, and he came over to my house. I thought this would be okay. I was getting a divorce.

Oh my God, I couldn't have been more wrong. Steve and I were making out on the couch heavily, and we were ready, very ready, to have sex; he was so hard. Suddenly, we heard a loud bang on the floor. It was my husband falling through the kitchen window. We jumped up, and Steve ran to the back of the house and out the window. Steve was scared shitless. I never heard from him again.

CRAIG: THE GUY NEXT DOOR (YUM)

Stan and I were divorced and just living together. I had to have the neighbor, Craig. He was so good-looking that every time I saw him I got wet with desire for him. I would see him across the street going in or out of his house, and he would smile at me! That was it. I had to have him.

Stan left for work at 5:00 a.m., and Craig and I arranged for him to come over and get into bed with me. The thought of having him was so exciting. When I talked to him, my clothes just wanted to fall off.

He knocked on the door after he saw Stan's car leaving my house. Thinking about what was about to happen was so hot. We went right to bed, and kissing his lips and feeling his hands all over me got me ready and excited. The thought nearly gave me an orgasm. I said, "I need you in me. Please put your cock in me."

To my shock, he had and was done.

I said, "What? Go inside."

He had and had already come. I could feel his come, but I'd I thought I was just really wet.

After all that, we were done. His dick was the size of my thumb. I couldn't believe that I couldn't feel it, not even a tickle. I felt sorry for him. He wanted to please me, but it was done. I did not have him back. What a letdown.

GUYS FROM THE THRIFTWAY STORE

Steve was a tall, lanky, eighteen-year-old kid who worked with me at Hank's Thriftway. His uncle owned the grocery store, and his brother worked there as well.

Steve and I flirted, and it was fun. Then the juices started flowing. I wanted to have sex with him. It was a cold desire, boring really. I just wanted to see what he was all about.

He was okay in bed, nothing to tell the world about.

Onto the next; Steve's uncle thought I would have sex with him. He was good-looking, but he was married. What a mess.

I worked with another guy, who also happened to be named Steve, whom I liked. He was going through a divorce. We would get together and talk and share companionship, along with great sex. He wanted to stay married, and he was trying to make it work. I really liked him.

That he wanted to stay with his wife was okay. I enjoyed that he was sharing some of his time with me. Oh boy, could he take care of my body. He kissed me well all over my body, and oral was out of this world. I could come over and over all night long, and he was long and nice to taste. You know, that is what made me want him more and miss him. He was very nice to me; that and the good sex made for a great combination. Of course, he did not have a shadow of asshole, so I just liked him.

CHAPTER FOUR

BUYING MY FIRST HOUSE

I N 1974, I BOUGHT MY first house. My new place was just up the street from my ex's place and near my kids' school. Stan stayed in the house we'd shared. He came over and looked at my house and commented that he had never had a house with a garage. I think he was thinking we were still together in a way. Well, I don't know what he was thinking. We were close because of the kids.

I filled the house with new furniture. But I would sell it within a year and move to Ohio—another time I acted without thinking.

NIGHT CLUBS AND GOOD-LOOKING GUYS WHO WERE MUSICIANS IN THE BANDS

Every time I went out, I would eye someone, and when I'd get his attention, all I knew was that he was thinking of me; I didn't realizing his thoughts were of sex only. I would get a man's attention, and I'd think, Wow, *he is looking at me*. He'd walk me to my car to talk, and sure, we'd talk. He liked me, right? That's why I got the attention. Then we'd have sex in the backseat of my car. Oh the many stories that seat could tell if it could talk. Of course, those men did not call or even want my phone number in the first place. I just did not get it! All I knew was that I felt alive inside. That was what I thought life was about. I walked away as if nothing had happened, my mind and heart cold, thinking, *This is okay; it's what life is about.* Boy, was I naive.

After the bars had closed, a group—sometimes the whole band, along with other girls—would end up going back to my house to party.

Each time I was with one of these men, I felt flattered. Was I an idiot? I know now how dumb and naive I was. We all know that I was not special in the eyes of those men. I just looked like I could be fucked. I did not realize this until years later.

A PORN STAR?

A friend of my sister's owned a porn store. Once when we were sitting in her living room, he asked me to join his group. He said I would be good at making porn. He explained that I could make good money and all I would have to do is be naughty and have fun. This is what I liked to do!

I laughed and told him that my ex was still taking care of me sexually and that he was good. I laughed so hard I fell back into a chair and flipped over the back of the chair.

I thought about his proposal. It *was* good money. In the end, I did not do it.

GUYS ON THE BEACH: MY FIRST VACATION AS A SINGLE GIRL

In 1974, I went to Hawaii with two of my girlfriends. This would be my first time in Hawaii and my first vacation. I was so excited.

Stan, who was still living with me, took me and my two girlfriends, Joyce and Kitty, to the airport. We were going for ten days. Wow, what an experience.

On our first day, the hotel where we were staying had a free continental breakfast for everyone and a show. I got up and got ready. I wanted to see and do everything. I had freedom—no ex to say no to me or tell me that I could not do things. *Freedom.* I woke my two girlfriends up and said, "Come on. Let's get ready and go."

They would not get out of bed; they were not interested. And that is how it was the entire ten days. Joyce and Kitty did eventually get up and drag themselves to the event.

I had fun right away. I was one of several girls to be grabbed and put on stage and sang to and, yes, flirted with. It was both embarrassing and a lot of fun.

During my entire stay in Hawaii, I felt like a princess—someone who had the whole world at her feet. I was on a high. We lay on the beach during the day and partied at night. So many good-looking guys were on the beach, and I got a lot of attention, I wasn't trying to; I just did.

My girlfriends were both average-looking and nice. I liked them.

I had so many experiences while I was in Hawaii. I met one guy at one of the shows that we bought tickets for. He was very good-looking—tall with a nice body—and came from a wealthy family. We met at the beach and talked and swam. He wanted me to stay in Hawaii so that we could continue seeing each other. He got me flowers. He was so complimentary to me.

Another of the guys I met was our tour guide. He made sure we had a great package and that he'd scheduled all the programs we'd signed up for. He was nice-looking, and we got hot and heavy. He got too serious, though, and became possessive. He wanted me to stay and live with him. And he came close to stalking me. He said that, when in Hawaii, neither girls nor men wore underwear. So I didn't.

I was there to enjoy my vacation and the men and people I met. I got a very dark tan and my hair was to my waist, so tourists would come up to me and ask for information, even though I was a haole.

CHAPTER FIVE

WEDDING NUMBER TWO

MIKE NUMBER ONE AND SECOND HUSBAND, 1976–1977

MIKE AND I HAD MET in Hawaii in 1974. He was a good-looking blond, and we were very attracted to each other. My girlfriends and I would lie on the beach every day. One day, two guys were lying next to us, and we started talking. Mike and Dave were very nice. We planned on doing things together. We rented a car and drove around seeing the sites. Mike and I started getting hot for each other in such a nice way. I felt I had met my prince. I wore my string bikini on the beach and little dresses out at night—with low backs and fronts too—and no underwear of course. We would dress up and go out and lay on the beach together. It was so romantic and such a high.

We talked about getting together after we left. He lived in Ohio, and we knew we wanted to meet to see where our budding romance would go. After I got home, Mike and I planned for me to fly out and see him. It was great.

A couple of days before I flew out, I went to get my hair shaped like Farrah Fawcett's. My hair hung to my waist, and I loved it. I was at the salon I'd selected, a place called The White House on Sandy Boulevard. I'd gone to several places to make sure the place I chose would do what I wanted with my hair. I was nervous. I explained again what I wanted, and of course the stylist insisted she could do it.

As she was, I thought, shaping my hair, I heard a few people go, "Ooooh."

Then the girl said, "Here's what's left. Should I cut it or not?" She was holding a strip of hair that was so short it made no difference or not whether she cut it. My hair was gone. She'd cut it short, and it now fell just to my shoulders. I went home crying.

When I was in first grade, my mom had stood me on a stool and cut my hair from waist-length to a bowl cut. I'd sobbed for days then, and now I was just as upset. But what could I do?

"It'll grow back," the stylist said. "This looks good."

Who was she? She did not have the right to cut my hair off. I was so naive. I just paid her and went home and cried.

The night before I was to fly out, my sister and I went to see the movie *Deep Throat*. Oh my God, I had never in my life seen an ex-rated movie—not like that. I was so hyped up sexually to see Mike. And during the flight, I read a book called *The Happy Hooker: My Own Story* by Xaviera Hollander, a book about a madam. Talking about being all sexed up and ready, I read the whole book.

When I landed, I was ready to rape Mike. He wasn't sure what was going on. I had just watched a triple X-rated movie the night before and had read a book all about sex that left nothing to the imagination. I think I slid off the plane. We were making out in the car, and I wanted Mike in me in the parking lot. He was reserved but wanted to be wild.

We made it to his place, and—look out—off with the clothes. Wow, it was so good, I mean great. He was fantastic in bed. He turned me every way but loose. Well, maybe it was me turning him every way but loose. His kissing was amazing, and so were his lips on my clit. He licked and sucked like I'd never experienced before. He was on top of me, behind me, and on my side. Our bodies just knew what to do together. I had seven or eight orgasms.

I lay in the sun while he worked, and I met his parents and family. They were extremely nice people and such a great family.

Mike asked me to marry him, and I said yes. I flew back home and started planning the wedding. As I looked for a dress and sold my home, I kept thinking, *How am I going to live away from my kids?* I couldn't. Something did not feel right.

When I was with Mike in Ohio and we would go look at wedding things and rings, I would wind up in the hospital with hives. Yes, every time I went to look at wedding rings or anything else related to the wedding, I would get terrible hives in my mouth and throat. The doctors would give me shots to help me. What kind of a sign was that? There was no bigger sign that I was feeling something wrong. Something was trying to tell me something.

I went to a psychologist, and she said I'd better think about my decision to marry Mike. Obviously, this did not seem like something I was supposed to do.

Still, I kept planning the wedding, and Mike and his family put it all together in Ohio.

Again, where was my brain? Between my legs? I thought only men had two heads and got confused between the two. Well, obviously, I would continuously think with my clit, with my cunt that was always wet. When sex rules all, how confusing life gets. You have sex and its good and you figure it must be love. Where in the hell is the logic in that?

Mike lived in Ohio. I lived in Oregon, and my young children lived here in Oregon.

We got married in December 1976. Mike drove up from Ohio to Portland, Oregon, to get me. We stayed at my ex's; I'll bet you don't see that one often.

The wedding was absolutely beautiful; the pictures were like a dream.

And then I just sat down and cried. I wanted to go home. I couldn't live so far away from my kids. I wasn't just living in a different town; I was in an entirely different state.

In February, my mom and dad called to wish me happy birthday and to say that they were sorry they could not send me a gift. Money was short. Dad was not feeling well. That was the sixteenth of February.

On February 22, I got another call. My dad had had a heart attack and passed away. I dropped to my knees and started bawling. I was all the way here in Ohio. I took the next flight out to go home. This was such a sad day to lose my dad.

One time, I wanted to go home to see my kids, and I just took off in my car and drove back to Oregon. I stayed with my sister, who was not always nice. But I would get dressed up and go out with friends to nightclubs and out dancing. What was wrong with this picture? I drove home to see my kids, and then my body took over. A pattern was here, but I couldn't see it yet. Nor could I feel the difference. I just was there with my kids, and sex took over and I just left them. Sex came first. Not good!

RICK: THE SKI BOAT MAN, 1977

You would think I was not married. My kids and I went to the river with my sister and her kids. A guy who'd come out with his boat started talking to us. He took all the kids and my sister out for a ride. I just lay in the sun.

When they came back, he asked me to dinner. He was good-looking and had a nice, sexy body. I was married and here with my kids. I thought to myself that I should say no. But I said yes. I met him that night, and after a fun dinner, we went back to his place and had wild, great sex. I don't understand it. I thought nothing of leaving my kids, who I was here to visit. And I was out getting attention. Was this a need or what?

I had to leave, and the drive home took me on long stretches of road. At one point in a long, long stretch of road, I was bored. I'd always wondered what it would be like to make myself have an orgasm. I'd never wanted to try before. I had read about it of course in books, like Xaviera Hollander's. So I propped my left knee tightly against the door and put my right hand in my pants. I found my clit and started to play. Whoa. It was good, and I was feeling this working, so I played and rubbed my clit until I had a great orgasm. After that, it seemed I was playing with myself everywhere I drove. I was addicted.

FREEWAY MAN

I was driving another long stretch the next day. I noticed a car that drove behind me, beside me, and sometimes in front of me. It seemed we were playing cat and mouse. We both pulled off the freeway at the same time and pulled up into the same gas station.

The driver and I met and talked and agreed to meet at a hotel and share a room for the night. I never thought anything of it. I'd never cheated on my first husband and did not think that I was the cheating type. Well, of course, there I went again; I was not thinking, and the clit had its own mind. We got a room and called our significant others. We had great sex, and off we went in the morning, each our own way.

I got back, and it could have been a great life, but I knew I needed to go home to Oregon. I called Stan and told him I needed to come home. I asked if I could live with him, and he said yes. I packed my things, got in my car, got home, and filed for a divorce.

I did fly back once later to see Mike. He said he wanted to wine and dine me, to make me feel good, so I would stay. I had a great time. It was nice seeing the friends I had met there. It was just that, when Mike picked me up at the airport, his hair was sticking out on the sides, and he looked like a Dutch painter boy. I'm a visual person, and the look turned me off. I got past it and had a good time. The sex was better than ever; I had so many orgasms. He kissed, sucked, and licked me every way possible. Yum.

CHAPTER SIX

New Encounters

After I went home to Oregon, I moved in with my ex and went back to work grocery checking at Thriftway.

Every year in May, I went to Hawaii.

Soon, I bought my second house on 124th and Sherman. I loved having my own home.

At one point, I had two guy roommates, and we all worked together at the store. Of course, they were both younger than me. One had a crush on me and wanted to date me.

No, I did not ever have sex with my roommates. Yes, I did make out with both of them, hoping the other did not know. Emery and I did make a date once without telling our other roommate; he would have been so hurt. We decided not to date, and it was better that way.

I had a big house and volunteered my house for the Thriftway Christmas party. I invited my mom and her husband. The guys made chocolate brownies for the party. We all had so much fun, and the evening went over well with our boss and all the employees.

The next morning, I had a physical therapy appointment. When I was ready to leave, I opened a cupboard and discovered some leftover brownies, so I put wrapped up two and put them in my purse. In the car, opened my purse up started eating the brownies—yum. Halfway to my doctor's office, I was feeling weird and spacey; my vision was off. I made it to the parking lot, which was across the street. I got out of my car and was not sure how I would get across the street.

I made it into the office, and the whole time I was there, I apologized for not feeling well. I'm sure they knew what was going on. I was trying to hide what was really going on with me. I do not think it worked.

When I left, I made it to my car and could not wait to get home and lay down until the dizziness passed. I told my roommates what had happened, and of course, they explained that I'd eaten "special" brownies, which were loaded with pot. I'd had two big ones; it's a wonder I'm not still feeling it. It was my first and only experience with pot. I did not like it and never wanted anything like it again.

TOM: THE MAN WITH CLASS

I went to Hawaii in 1987 and met Tom on the beach. Tom was extremely good-looking, and he was classy and had money. He lived in Newport Beach, California. I was attracted to his black hair; blue eyes; and, my favorite, great body. We talked a lot.

He only had a few days left in Hawaii when I met him. I did go back to his room, and he had a roommate, so we just talked all night sitting on the floor. He invited me to California to see him. Of course, when I got home, he called and bought me a ticket to fly out and see him. I was very excited and nervous.

In California, we went to a very expensive restaurant, where we sat high up with a great view of the city. We would go to the beach and lay in the sun. We both had dark tans.

I went to see him several times, and once, while lying on the beach, he asked if I might have his child. He had no children and thought I was perfect. *What a compliment*, I thought. And I was shocked.

I know I usually start off telling about the sex. Well, I am getting to it. Tom kissed extremely well. I would get so turned on, and he felt very good. I loved being with him. He was such a classy man, a true gentleman. However, every time I visited him, he would, of course, try and make me have an orgasm, and I couldn't. I don't know why.

One time, I faked it. I just felt so bad for him; he tried so hard for me to have an orgasm. I just had to try and fake it. I'm sure he knew. I told him it was a little one but that I had come. I had my fingers crossed. I felt so bad lying to him, even though it was a little fib.

We stayed in touch for a couple of years. I had already met Mike when Tom and I were getting together, and I would call Tom even when I was first visiting Mike in Ohio. Then I did decide to just see Mike ... well sort of. *Shame on me.*

MARK: THE RED LION'S BAR MANAGER

I checked groceries during the day and cocktailed at the Red Lion in Vancouver at night. As a cocktail waitress, I made good money. We wore short, short skirts and low-cut tops; the outfits were cute.

The manager at Red Lion, Mark, was good-looking and had a great personality. He was married. I worked at the restaurant for a year, and the manager was always flirting. I did not flirt back because another waitress liked him and wanted him, married or not. The slut!

One night, I was about ready to finish my shift and Mark came to me and said he'd left something for me in the check-out room. He told me to look for it when I got off work while I was counting my money out. The waitress who liked him was counting out at the same time.

Yes, our boss had a bottle of champagne waiting, along with a note and a room number. Was I flattered? No. He was married.

I went to the room, but I did not have sex with him. The next day,

I went into the office and told him I quit. He followed me down the hall and said that was not necessary. Another job and more sexual harassment.

THE WILLIE NELSON LOOK-ALIKE

I met a guy through a friend who worked on foreign cars. I had a 240Z, and I was looking for someone to work on my car. The mechanic and I became friends. We would hang out at his house while he worked on my car. He also went to the Grand Old Opry and won the Willie Nelson look-alike contest. What fun.

We did not have sex, but we would sleep together. What can I say? Usually when I had a body against me, it was just natural to have good, old sex. But I didn't with him. I don't know why I did not go there. Somehow he felt different for me.

KURT: FROM THE WEST SIDE

I was out at a bar in Portland on the river when I met Kurt and he asked me out. Kurt lived on the west side, and I had a home on the east side. Thanks to Kurt, I had my first experience with the difference between Portland's west side in crowd and their thoughts about east side people.

Kurt was nice to talk to and look at. Sex was great, and we went at it every way but loose. His tongue was all over me, from head to toe and in the middle. Wow, the kissing turned me on; I got so wet just being with him. We really would work up a sweat. Our bodies would be hot and wet all over from our play. Our chemistry was incredibly good. It had better be.

I will never forget the time when he told me that he had never gone out with anyone who lived on the east side. He thought I was great, and he had been missing out. He said he had not thought that east side girls had class or could be good-looking. Heaven forbid, a woman should live on the east side of town. I guess I changed his mind.

MIKE NUMBER TWO: ALL ABOUT SEX

Mike was a pararescue specialist for the #304th Pararescue squadron at the local air base. He was not someone I would look at and want to go out with, but we met and hit it off. He was physically in shape and kept in shape for his work. I loved keeping in shape. I ran around Glendoveer Golf Course three times, which was around six miles three times a week. Between that, aerobics, and sex all night, I was in good shape.

Mike and I would go out to dinners. I did compulsively eat. He would ration the amount I could eat—not nice.

We had great sex. He was a great lover, and the size of his cock was perfect—long and thick—to go into me just to fuck me. Yes, thank you, honey. You made me crave you! Mike really knew how to take care of my body, and this is and was the one thing that mattered to me in the beginning of dating any man and the reason for my relationships. Right?

We would work up a sweat every time we had sex. His body was nice and firm, and he had the right amount of black hair on his body and chest. He had black hair and blue eyes, my favorite combination. I never could get enough of him.

He was nice to date, and we got kind of serious. He did ask me whether I would go with him if he got transferred to another state. I said no, and our relationship was never the same. I was not focused on him.

One night I was supposed to meet him, and I went to have one drink after work with the girls at Refectory, next door to the Thriftway where I worked. I did not watch the time, and I was late by the time I left. I went to Mike's and said I was sorry, explaining that I had lost track of the time. He was mad. He said he'd come to the bar and watched me, laughing and having fun and not respecting him and our time and the date we had. We stayed friends.

Mike went on a trip out of the country to climb a mountain, Mt.

Everest. While he and his climbing partners were still climbing, it was getting dark and a storm came up. They had to stop and squat on a ledge to sleep. When they started to climb in the morning, his toes were frozen. When he came home, he went right to the hospital. His toes were black. He had to have his toes cut off. Mike had to learn to walk again. I was in the hospital with him. The girl he was seeing at the time was there too. My ex, Stan, came to see him also. He wanted to help Mike. That was nice.

Mike was very glad I was there, and so was I. Again, the sex was good, but he had never had kids, and we had different ideas on life.

Who am I kidding? I had no idea what a real relationship was about. I guess and know now that I had a lot to learn. And, in time, I would, as I could have been guided all the way, if I listened to my inner voice. But then this story could not have been told.

A few years later, Mike was coming into town and called me. I told him I was working and that he should come in and see me. I was cocktailing at night at Steamers on 82nd. He did come in, and it was very nice to see him.

The guy I was seeing, who was living with me, had just come in and left. I knew in the back of my mind that he was cheating and that he lied to me. Why was I with him? Was I needy? Did I, like many men, have to have a body? I did not know.

Mike asked me to come to his hotel room after work. I said okay; it would be nice to talk. Who am I kidding?

As soon as I got to the room, the clothes came off. I do not regret it; he felt so good. And he genuinely liked me and cared for me. I never heard from him again. I've always wondered if he ended up getting married and having a child.

RICK AND HIS KNOTTY COCK

I had seen Rick in high school when I was a freshman. My sister knew him and had gone out with him a few times. He was one of the nice, wild, good-looking guys in school. I ran into him at a party ten years later. He asked if we could get together, and we did.

Rick was a very nice guy, and he had been married also. He had a home in SE Portland not far from mine. I liked getting together with him for sex. The first time, I was scared or shocked to discover that his dick had knots all over. I tried to be cool, but it looked like a bad disease. He assured me it was okay, nothing catching, just a flaw.

I did not go down on him. I could not get the knots out of my mind. I needed to move on. He was such a nice guy too. Anyway, I was just using him to fill my sexual needs, I guess.

Even though I'd left my ex-boyfriend Mike, he had been lying in my bed with his toes all gone from frostbite, and I had been taking care of him for a week. I thought I had to go out for a night so I could have sex again. I was sick and thoughtless, just into myself and my needs. I did not feel I was doing anything wrong. I just looked at going out for sex like going to the store for chocolate. Remember, my chest did not feel; only my cunt did. It was so sad, the learning.

PAUL: THE PRODUCE GUY

I had a crush on Paul, just a little one. He was blond and blue-eyed and very nice-looking. He was also nice to be with, and he was good in bed. We did our own thing, but we were friends and liked to talk to each other. We would go to lunch together, which turned out to be a problem at work.

One day, Doug, the manager of the store, who had worked for the company for thirty years, called me into the office. He said he had a friend who he wanted me to meet. The friend would be coming by the store that day, and the manager wanted me to go to lunch with him. He said his friend was a very nice guy and he thought we should meet and date. He was not asking me; he was telling me.

Later, I saw a tall man go into the manager's office, and then I was called into the office. After Dave and I had been introduced, the manager told us to go have lunch and take our time and talk.

Everyone in the store, especially the checkers, was looking at me. It was not my lunchtime, and I was leaving the store.

Dave and I walked over to the little restaurant next door and talked. He asked me out, and I said maybe. He was nice and okay-looking, but I was not attracted to him.

When I got back and walked into the store, I felt a cold feeling. The checkers were giving me a stare down. The tension was high.

Dave came back to the store. He came through my check stand to say hi and ask me out. I had decided that I was not getting together with him.

One day, I was out to lunch with Paul, and when we got back, we were both called into the office one at a time. I was written up for being late and told to not go to lunch with Paul. The manger wanted me to go out with his friend and was making it difficult for me at the store. Paul was also told not to go to lunch with me.

My boss came into the lunchroom and said that Dave was a nice guy and I should have a date with him.

Dave called, and we got together. He helped me with my first résumé.

I quit my job at the store. I could not take the manager's pressure and manipulation anymore. There I went again, just walking away. I should have reported the manager. I have too many should have's. I quit so many jobs because managers wanted to control my life sexually.

MIKE NUMBER THREE: SO GOOD-LOOKING WITH BLACK HAIR AND BLUE EYES

Tequila Willies was a bar on the Willamette River that was very popular with the in crowd. For a few years, I went to Willies every Friday. One Friday, I was sitting at a tall bar table, and five or six people were sitting at a table in front of the window, several good-looking guys among them. I just kept staring at two of them—a blond and another guy with coal black hair and blue eyes.

At one point, the blond came over to the table with another guy, who turned out to be his brother. The blond was a chiropractor. He was very good-looking. I was with just one of my girlfriends, and we all started to talk. I still wanted to meet the guy with the black hair, who was five foot eleven. Well, we all started talking, and we had fun. I should have gone for the blond. He was nice and real, but it was obvious I wanted to meet their friend.

Eventually, the friend came over to the table; he thought the party must be at our table. The blond and his brother introduced me, and his name was Mike. There I went again. I wanted him. He was good-looking—tall and sexy with that bad-boy look. We talked, and he asked me out.

Mike ran around with the in crowd. All of his friends were good-looking, and they worked hard and partied harder.

Mike and I met several times, and then he started staying at my house. I had a house, and he lived in an apartment with a roommate. He snow skied and had a cabin at Government Camp with six other guys. I started to go up there every weekend with him. I had so much fun.

Everyone thought we were about sex. We were always in bed, and he did know how to please my body and that was not easy. My clit is tilted upward, so in order to have an orgasm, I have to place myself just right on the man's pelvic bone so I can rub against it. It was so nice when one fit and was a willing participant. So I guess that is why I just went for it if a man could please me; I thought that must mean it was love. Isn't that what we all think?

Okay, again with the clit. The world revolved around the clit.

We had a lot of fun. Mike had a lot of friends. He was insecure. He always made comments putting me down. I knew what he was doing, so I just allowed it because I had a house and a nice car. I did somewhat well for myself. He just wasn't secure with himself. This kind of man belittles a woman in order to make himself feel better. I was secure with myself, so I just made myself bigger than what was said; and if criticizing me made him feel better, I just let it go. Who was the dumb one again?

Mike decided to move in with me. I had two other roommates as well. Mike gave his roommate a thirty-day notice. He told me he gave his roommate rent for the next month. In truth, he didn't. He just didn't want to pay me for the first month. I only charged him three hundred dollars for a month's rent. I paid six hundred. Oh well, he took me, and he was cheap. Maybe he needed the money to party with. I let it go again.

Living with Mike was great. We had a yard sale, and he was right there, involved and sitting with us. I was so attracted to him. The kids liked him. My daughter went to work for him at a clothing store at Clackamas Town Center for a while. That was nice.

One day, Mike called and said he was leaving work and going straight up to the mountains. I thought this was odd; he never did this. I got suspicious. I called into work—I worked at UPS now driving a truck—and said I could not make it in. I got my sister, and we drove up to the mountains that night.

When we arrived, Mike looked at me and said, "See, no one is with me."

I still did not like what was going on. Something about the situation wasn't right. But he was alone.

My sister and I went back down the mountain and headed home.

Shortly after that, Mike and I parted, and he moved out.

When I got a Porsche a little while later, I drove up to the mountains. I knew he would be there. I showed him my car, and he just acted upset. "Of course you would have a Porsche," he said. "Do you get everything you want?"

"I work hard for what I get," I told him.

He did not get it. The Porsche was something else for him to feel insecure about.

Later down the road, we started talking about maybe getting

back together. I wasn't seeing anyone, but I had someone I was seeing for sex and thought I should meet him and tell him that I was getting back together with my ex-boyfriend. So one night, on my way to meet Mike, I stopped and had a drink with my friend to tell him what was going on.

I was a little late getting to Mike's, and he just kept questioning me. I said I had been at my mom's, and he had me call my mom. Of course, it was a lie, but I knew he could not handle the truth. So that was that again with us.

We talked some more, and I tried to explain what was happening. He just got upset. He wanted me, but he also wanted something else—who knows what?

A FIRE IN THE HOUSE?

I happened to meet a guy who was visiting up the street, and the two of us hit it off. We made a date and came back to my place to have wild, passionate sex. We were kissing and playing, and I was so wet. He was nice to look at naked and had a good-sized cock and a great body I could have an orgasm just looking at him. We got into it really hot and heavy and were soon having wild, passionate sex. We were both wet from head to toe.

The phone rang, and I did not pick it up. But it kept ringing and ringing, so I answered it. It was Mike. I was surprised. I had wanted to be with him and just see him. But I would not be toyed with. I was breathing heavy and trying to be cool. Mike kept asking me if someone was there. I kept saying no, and he kept saying yes there is. I finally said yes. He went crazy, and I hung up.

The guy from up the street and I went back to having the best, wildest sex, every way but loose. It was so, so good. We were having it with him coming from behind, not anal; I never did that. My ass was in the air. We had sixty-nine, and we were moaning and yelling, "Yes." We were sweating. We were hot and wet.

All of a sudden, the doorbell rang, and I saw lights flashing outside the window. I answered the door. Oh my God, I never would have guessed. Five fire trucks were parked outside my door. The firemen said someone had called and said there was a fire at this house.

I assured the men that there was no fire in or around this house. *Maybe in the bedroom*, I thought but kept the thought to myself. "I'm sorry," I said. "I do not know who would have called you because it is just me and my friend here."

It was obvious that I was having sex. My hair was wet, and I was flushed from being so hot!

Once the firemen had looked around and determined that there was, indeed, no fire, they left. When I went back into the bedroom, I could see that I had not put the phone all the way back into the receiver and the line was still connected.

Apparently, Mike had been screaming to hang up, and I guess he'd heard all the sexual noises and was going crazy to make it stop. Not knowing what else to do, he'd called the fire department to come stop us. I did not leave the line connected on purpose, but it did serve him right.

From then on, when I would see Mike at the mountains, I would talk to everyone and never look at him. I would act like he wasn't even in the room.

MIKE NUMBER FOUR: A MILLIONAIRE

Mike was a nice-looking, professional guy who wore nice suits. He did well for himself. We had met several times at the bars in downtown Portland where the in crowd went. He always said hi and flirted, but he never asked me out.

Mike did very well for himself. He had a home in Lake Oswego on the lake. I have to mention him because he never asked me out when I lived on the east side of Portland. Once I'd bought a home on the west side, I guess I was datable? We went out a few times. He was funny and fun to be with. We became friends—yes, with benefits.

Sex was fun. He was always thoughtful of my needs and pleasing me. We laughed and played sexually. His cock was yummy, and his lips kissing me all over were nice too. One time, he said to me, "You bought this house. You must have something like $150,000 in equity." He was implying that I was now okay to date. I was insulted. He thought I was getting classy because I lived on the west side now and had equity. Now he could date me or marry me. I always had fun with him, but it was obvious that, if I still lived on the east side of Portland and did not have a house on the west side, he wouldn't consider me dateable.

Mike pursued me for years. He wanted me to go to a place called Ace of Hearts on the east side of town. This is a place where you go and have sex with other people or groups. I had never seen anything like this and was not interested. I had a good friend who I hung out with who went to Ace of Hearts and had often invited me to join in. Nope, I wasn't going there. My friend and Mike thought that, since I was so sexual, I would enjoy all this. But, no, I like putting all my sexual energy into one at a time behind closed doors—well, almost.

When I was dating Rudy, who had been born in Switzerland and frequented the red light district in Holland regularly, I'd agreed to go to the place one time just to look. I trusted Rudy to take me in to look. My friend had invited us there as guests. Oh my God. We were greeted by other couples who asked us to join them. We went to different floors and watched through glass windows scenes like two women having sex. One could, at any time, go join in. On one floor there were beds, and on another, men and women were sitting on couches while someone was eating or sucking on them—oral all the way.

This was all too much for me. We went all through the place and danced a couple dances and left. Now I knew what these places were all about. Not my cup of tea.

Mike also mentioned that he and his friends liked to take a boat out and wear no clothes and have fun with each other. *I* was worthy to date *him* because I lived on the west side. Who was worthy or not?

Later on, I heard him telling some friend that we were trying to date and that we had something to work out. Little did he know, I was not trying.

He was a millionaire, but he was cheap—very cheap! He never asked if he could buy me a drink at any time throughout the time we met or were together, and when we went out to dinner, it was to places like Denny's. He had a million-dollar house and was cheap. Now do you think I would be attracted to all that? I don't think so. I never was, and I was never going to be. He never understood why I did not go there with him—why we didn't become a couple.

He never understood that his idea of fun turned me off. I felt he had no class and was sick. He felt my rejection was hurtful, and for years, he wouldn't talk to me. Oh well.

Then I ran into him at the Museum After Hours, an event every Wednesday with music and drinks; it was a gathering for singles, and everyone went. Mike did say hi and asked me to come over and meet his wife. How nice of him. She was a very pretty little gal, well dressed, and of course, she had money.

After he introduces me to her, which was nice, we stepped away, and he told me his wife thought I was nice and had suggested inviting me over to their house. I was flattered. Then Mike said, "I mean she really liked you."

I still said, "That is nice."

He explained that she liked me and wanted to get together with me while Mike watched. He smiled and laughed, knowing this was not me. He still thought he would try again with me. It made me sick.

BOB NUMBER ONE: A MILLIONAIRE

In 1976, Bob had five grocery stores. I worked for him as a checker at his Thriftway store in Fairview. Bob would always call me. Sometimes I would meet him for a drink and talk. Once, he called me early in the morning to say he had a ticket for me to go someplace with him and his managers for the weekend, adding that he knew someone who could get me the weekend off. I never went. This went on for years.

Bob was married for twenty years to Patty, and the two of them had a daughter they had adopted. He was such a player. He was funny and fun to talk to, but he was married.

When he got a divorce, we went out and drank a bottle of champagne. We went to a golf tournament party, a gathering for the pros. We never had sex. I did not want sex with him. For one thing, his breath was the worst I had ever been around. So I could not get close to him.

He tried, but nope, I was not going there at all, no matter how much money he had.

Once I got a call from Bob. He wanted to meet for a drink. He was married for the second time and was unhappy. I did not know he had been married again. Now, he was going through a divorce. She wanted to live higher and more lavishly than he did. She liked to spend his money. We met and talked and that was that.

Later in the years, Bob called and said he was bringing his canoe up the Willamette River to the riverfront and wanted to know if I would join him and some friends for a little gathering. I said yes. He'd said other people were going to be there, and I felt that was good and safe, since I never knew if he was married or not.

I got to the riverfront, and wow, his "canoe" was a sixty-foot yacht named *Golden Eagle*. On the yacht, I met a friend of Bob's. Carl was a pharmacist, and he was very nice and nice to talk to. He invited me to meet him sometime. As we were talking and Bob was busy, I asked Carl how many people would be joining us. Carl said no one and that he was leaving too. I said, "Oh really?"

At one point in our conversation Carl said that Bob's girlfriend— well, his fiancée—was on a world bike tour. Bob had gotten me again with his lies.

Carl left; Bob and I had a glass of wine while he cooked us

dinner. It was a nice evening, and we attempted to make out. But as you know, I just wasn't into him, money or no money. I was upset after Carl told me that Bob was engaged. I left feeling hurt again. Sometime it would be good to have someone just be honest.

Bob was attracted to me for years and always attempted to date or do me. I would later hear that he did get married for the third time. More about Bob later on in the book; and it just gets worse!

DAN: THE OWNER OF A FLOATING HOME MOORAGE

I was out with the girls when I met Dan, one of the guys about town who always said hi. He was known to be wild and on drugs, and rumor had it that he maybe even sold them. He liked coke, and he had money. He wasn't bad-looking either.

One night, he asked if I wanted to go to another bar to party with his friends. I never did this, but he convinced me and I said okay. I would take my car and follow them.

As I was following, I realized that they were not headed to the bar. I asked what was going on. Dan explained that they had to stop at his house and pick up something. I did not like the idea but followed anyway. He said that I should come in, assuring me it would only take a minute.

I did, and they got the coke out and not the drink. I had never tried the stuff and never planned to, and I wasn't up for sitting around and watching this either. I was so upset. I had been set up. Was I just an idiot and completely naive? Or maybe I just trusted because I wanted so much to believe people's word. Yes, that was it!

Then Dan and his friend wanted me, so we made out on the bed. I was too nervous to enjoy myself. They suggested that we get into the shower. It was fun. I was scared, not sure if I would be hurt or raped. They played; they both had great hard-ons. Their bodies were nice, and they were being so sweet. I liked it but did not want to be there. Then why was I still there? I think I was just out of my body, and the situation had an element of excitement. I was still too aware and wanted to stay aware of what was going on so nothing stupid would happen.

We went back to the bed. I said I would have sex with one but not two of them, just to change the situation. (As if I would have really had sex with either one of them.) I had to leave. I was never as mad as I was when I realized what these guys were about and that I'd let them talk me into their trap. I would never acknowledge him and his friend again out and about. Sexual perverts!

MARK: THE THIEF

I had signed up for a 10K run in Portland, and I was at the race with my friend, Kathy, and her husband. A guy who they knew from work came up to us to say hi to them. He was in terrific shape. We talked, and he asked me out. I thought, *This could be nice.* So I said okay. Where's the crystal ball when you need one? If only we could look ahead.

Mark and I started to date, and ours was the wildest sex I'd ever had. He was about sex too. Oh boy, did he know a woman's body. He was great at fucking, and when it came to oral, his tongue was the best. He had a nice-sized cock; actually it was perfect. I loved going down on him and sucking every drop out of his oh-so-hard cock. He could take care of my body, and as you know, that was what life was about—making sure we have all the orgasms and all the passion we want. At least that was what I thought life was about. I did not know the difference between sex and love yet. I thought feeling through sex was natural. I didn't know that life had so much more to offer. I would find out the difference a lot of years later. At least I found out. Yeah!

At one point during our dating, I started to feel like something was wrong. Why can't we listen to our great inner voices, which are watching out for us? I didn't; I figured I knew better.

I decided to drive over to his apartment to talk to him. I knew something was wrong. As I drove up, I saw him and a young girl. He had her hand, and he tried to sneak into his apartment.

I knocked on his door and kept knocking until he answered it. The girl came to the door too. Yes, they were together. She was living in his apartment, and he was seeing me and her at the same time.

I went home and took his name-brand jeans, shoes, and shirts and put them in the fireplace and burned them. Now who was the dumb one? Still me. Later, I would find out that he had stolen his clothes from the stores and that he changed the tags also.

After that, I still had him move in after he explained to me what the situation really was. I said okay, but I did not feel right about my decision.

Mark had a son, and I would take him places with me. Mark would take my son places as well. He was a runner, so we ran together all the time. At one point, Mark asked me to marry him. I said yes.

This was one time when I did get my brain out of my cunt and thought, *This is not good.* I had sent out invites to fifty guests. Now I called every one and explained that I was not getting married but I would have a big party, a barbecue. Wow, that was a close. Among the hundreds of things I had done without feeling right about them, I had stopped myself from going through with this one at least; this was a start.

I did get pregnant. I wanted to have another child but not his. I had an abortion. This was hard. I was okay doing it; I just would dream of this child trying to find him.

I never felt good about what Mark said. I knew he was not being truthful. He once said he had to go to Eugene for a weekend for a meeting at the 24 Hour Fitness; he worked there part-time. He said he would have to stay the night, as the drive back was too long. I looked at him and said, "I don't think so. There will never be days like that." I said that he could not go and stay a night.

Finally, one night I got off early from work. I never left work until 2:00 a.m. and didn't usually get home until 2:30. I typically stayed on until close because that was where the last good money was. But on this night, I headed home around 1:00 a.m.

I drove home, and when I went into the house, Mark wasn't there. I took off my uniform and nylons, and then it hit me. *He is not home,* I told myself. *Get your clothes back on.* I changed back into my uniform and nylons. I went out, locked the house, got in my car, and drove down the street. I turned off the car and sat there without the lights on facing my house.

At 2:20, a car with the headlights on turned into my driveway. Mark was home. I waited twenty more minutes so that I would arrive home at my normal time. I pulled up into the driveway, went in to the house, and said, "Hi," adding, "oh sorry to wake you."

Mark was in bed with the TV on. I started to undress again. He said that he had been watching a movie and must have fallen asleep, and then he went on telling me about the movie. Well, we know he wasn't watching it in this house. The asshole!

I put on my nightgown and crawled into bed. Mark asked, "Is everything okay?"

I said, "Yes, I'm just tired. Why?"

"I know there is something wrong," he replied.

I was trying to be cool and not say anything and do the same thing I would do every night. Why was he asking? "I don't know," I said. "Why do you ask, honey?"

"Well," he said, "you have a nightgown on, and you never come to bed with anything on."

I could not believe I hadn't thought of this. I just knew I was feeling dirty and sick. I knew I had caught him in a big lie. All this time, I had felt something was up, and this time, I'd checked out what was going on to make sure that my feeling was justified; and I'd been right.

Your inner voice is usually right; if you feel something, you should listen. Mark and I went to sleep after I told him I would talk to him about it later; he would not let it go. He always tried so hard to please, and now I knew he did it to cover up what he was doing behind my back. He had something to hide, and that is why he wondered what I knew—why I would think he would do anything wrong. I said it was a feeling and that I believed in my feelings.

A few days went by, and he was going to take a tree stump out for me. Mark was so worked up trying to figure out what I was thinking; it drove him nuts. I told him that after he'd taken out the stump we would talk.

Jeez, he was worked up; he couldn't wait to hear what I had to say. He took the big stump out in a few hours. It was amazing to watch.

When he was done, we went into the family room, and he sat on the couch. I said, "Mark, I have a lot to say, and I want to say it. I'm going to swear and yell and when I am done, I want to go about the rest of the day and enjoy it. But do not get mad. I am going to really tell it like it is."

I straddled his lap. I started out, "You fucker." I pointed my finger and added, "You lying son of a bitch." I told him again not to get mad but to listen to what I had to say. Then I went on to tell him how I'd come home early and discovered he was not home and how I'd gone down the road and waited. I knew that everything he'd said—about where he was and who he was with—was a lie. I called him every name in the book, and he had nothing to say; he'd been caught red-handed.

This was enough; we went and had a good rest of the day. I, of course, could not deal with the situation anymore. He moved out.

But the story about him just gets better. I wondered where he lived, but he would not say. I asked the mailman for Mark's new address, and he told me. I know he was not supposed to, but he did. The reason I asked the mailman where I could find Mark was that, after Mark moved out, I had a break-in at my home. My water bed had been cut, and so had my roommate's. I had money in the mattress, and it was gone, along with some of the clothes from my closet and some of my underwear. The thief had picked out certain clothes and underwear; it was odd. The glass in the window by the back door was broken, and whoever it was had taken my microwave and two TVs.

The police came. Mark was there, showing the officers that he'd found pot above the garage—a weird place. And how would Mark have known it was there? He wasn't living there; it was odd. He said he thought my son had something to do with this. Something was fishy, and my son wasn't involved, even though he did get into trouble a lot. Mark was trying too hard to convince the police to put the blame on my son, and he looked weird doing this. You know that feeling.

After Mark left, that is when I asked the mailman for his address. I knew Mark stole my stuff. I went to his apartment, and he was not there; he had moved in with a girl. He had my things. I looked in the windows, and I could not see anything. I flattened his tires and tore the screens out of his windows.

I left a message saying that I knew he had taken my things. I ran into a friend of his later, and the friend said that Mark had stolen some things from him when he needed money. According to the friend, Mark just had this bad habit; he could not stop stealing. Mark had needed a place to live, and the friend had told Mark, "Do not steal from me, or I will put you in jail, and you will have no place to live." He'd told him to watch his Ps and Qs. What a lowlife. Now who was to blame? I'd seen the red flags. Was I a dummy? What was my problem? Was this all I was attracted to? I needed to start listening to my inner voice.

KENT: THE FABIO LOOK-ALIKE

I was sitting on a barstool, which I liked doing, ordering an appetizer at a bar in downtown Portland called The Pilsner. This guy who was sitting to the left of me started talking to me, and we hit it off.

Kent was nice-looking, and his story was a good one. What a life he'd had. He didn't drink. A big guy with long blond hair, he looked so much like Fabio they could have been brothers. He was a former drug addict and had kicked the habit. From the stories he told me, I gathered that he had been a mess. He cleaned up his act and studied and became a broker and was doing well for himself.

Kent and I became good friends. We would go to the movie theater where you could order food and drink or go lie on the beach. On Halloween, we would dress up—me in leathers and a whip and him in leathers and a spiked collar. We had fun going to the big parties, just as friends. We talked all the time. We had such a good friendship.

In the beginning, he wanted to have sex with me. Oh really! I decided why not; he was my friend, and I only wanted to have him as a friend. To me, this was so nice. He wouldn't invite me to his floating home, so he rented a motel room in a hotel with prostitutes standing outside. We tried to have sex, and he could not get it up. He was just too nervous, as he had wanted me so badly and waited so long full of desire.

I said, "We're friends. Let's just keep it this way."

I asked him not to overstep the boundaries. He would try, and I would remind him that we were only friends. One time, he pushed it so hard, trying to kiss me and go further than I wanted, that I stopped talking to him for nine months.

After that, we started talking again and hanging out together. I said trying for sex wasn't worth it because it stopped us from being friends, and he agreed. We liked talking and doing things together.

He eventually moved on got a girlfriend and moved to Hawaii. After that, we didn't talk anymore. I guess she was jealous.

CHAPTER SEVEN

THE LIGHT ACROSS HIS EYES

COCKTAILING: STEAMERS LOUNGE, 82ND AND SANDY

I WAS STILL CHECKING GROCERIES DURING the day and cocktailing at night so I could make better money. This was not a good setup for someone who had kids at home, but I liked bringing home a decent amount of money. I was working at Lamb's Thriftway in Fairview maybe four days a week, and my paycheck wasn't enough to pay the bills. So I got a job at Steamers as a cocktail waitress.

RAY, GOOD-LOOKING AND NICE AND THE ONE WHO CHANGED MY LIFE FOR GOOD: FIRST FEELINGS OF REAL LOVE

Working there would change a lot in my life; it would begin to mold how I thought and felt toward men. I would experience an awakening, in which I would learn much about what I could feel inside.

One night, the lounge was busy, and I was all over the place. I picked up a tray from the bar, and when I turned around to serve my drinks, I glanced up and to the right toward the seating above the dance floor and caught sight of a man seated at the end of the tables. As I looked at him, I said to myself, *That is the man I could be in love with.*

I looked at his face, and even though the lights were dim, I could see a light across his eyes. I thought the whole thing was odd, but somehow, I knew I could love this man. I let the feeling go. I went up the stairs to the left and served my drinks. Then I made my way around the top to the last stool where he was sitting, and I asked what he would like to drink. I got his drink, and when I came back, we started talking. He shared some stories about some pictures we had on the wall. His name was Ray, and he was a ship's captain.

I do not know what came over me, but I asked someone to dance with me, a man who was a good dancer. I wanted him to turn me and twirl me and move my body all around the floor. I wanted to tease and please Ray. I wanted to be sexy and move my body so that he would think of me all night. I finished my dance. I had never done that before, and dancing with customers was not allowed. I could get fired. I do not know why, but I had to dance and move to please the guy sitting up there.

Ray asked me out to breakfast when I got off work at 2:30 in the morning. I said yes. He was so good-looking, with his black hair and blue eyes. I put my thoughts of him when I'd first seen him in the back of my mind. I did not think anything of that first impression until later in the weeks to come. What a shock when I did.

For now, we went out. I mustn't forget the sex and lovemaking, which was out of this world. He made me feel every part of my body. We had sex in every position—from sixty-nine to him on top and from behind—except anal; yuck. His kisses were the best. I could have as many orgasms as I wanted. We fit so well. He looked, tasted, and felt just right—his way. I loved how he made me feel.

Shortly after the first time we got together, he was going to Kanata, so I got my kids and he had his son, and we met there. We would go out to nice dinners together and take the kids sometimes. We had so much fun.

He had a van and once, when we were shopping at a place on 82nd, which was a big shopping center then, we got back to the van and we just went for it in the van. I was in heaven. It was so wild and good, just downright great fucking. I got him a sticker for his van that said, "If this van is rocking, don't come knocking." Boy, was it rocking!

Once we were making dinner at his house in Rock Creek outside of Portland, we got to talking about his family. He told me about a time when his grandmother was in the hospital. Ray said his grandmother had told him that the woman who he would truly love would see a light across his eyes. I told him what I had seen the first time I had looked up and saw him and that I'd told myself that was the man I would love. We both had our breath taken away.

He stared at me, and we both just sat down to get our thoughts together. We knew we loved each other and started talking about our future. We planned a weekend together. He worked two weeks on and two weeks off.

The weekend arrived, and I got ready and drove to his place. When I got there, the door was open and I walked in. He was nowhere in sight. As I walked through the living room, I saw a nice, big fire going in the fireplace. To the left on the bar area as you entered the kitchen sat two brandy glasses with Baileys in them, my favorite. I was filled with the warmth of the love and caring and closeness we had. I was experiencing what it felt like to be in love.

You see, I had never been in love or felt this before. I had only known "love and caring" based on sex; of course, we all know that, when a guy has sex with us, it must be love, or caring at least. What a fool I had been. It was just sex.

Anyway, as I stood there with this great feeling, taking in the perfect atmosphere he had created, Ray was outside cutting firewood. Never had I ever experienced anything so special, and the feelings threw me off my guard. As I stood there in this very happy moment, I went from thinking about how I would be happy and life would be good to telling myself I would be bored. This life would be boring for me. I had never been happy, and I had only had roller-coaster rides for boyfriends. The bad boys—that was what I was used to. You knew where they were coming from. They lied to you and cheated on you. I couldn't handle this feeling of being in love. I had to ruin this. I could not give myself permission to be happy.

Why? What was it that I had to learn in my journey? Did I not deserve to be happy, to have someone love me, and to be in love?

For three months, I felt what it was like to be in love. Then something inside me took over, telling me to ruin this, and I started to back off. Ray could not understand. I called Mark, and we got together. I stood Ray up when I was supposed to meet him for a movie. I just flowed with whatever—not knowing what was right or wrong.

Ray knew that, when we'd first gotten together, I had just recently ended a relationship with a boyfriend who had been living with me and that I had asked him to move out. That was the best thing I ever did. Mark was a cheating, lying, stealing bastard. And then I called him. I got scared. I did not think about what I was doing; I just called Mark and had him come over. I sabotaged myself every time things might be good for me. Did I think I did not deserve to be happy? What was it that I was supposed to be paying for? What made me believe that I should be treated poorly?

Of course I called Ray and said I was sorry, that it was just him I wanted to be with. His feelings were so hurt that he would not let me in. I tried, but he could not get over his heart being hurt by me.

I ran into him at Bebop's and we said hi. I looked at him, and as I placed my hand over his heart, I said, "Your heart was hurt, and now you can't let me in."

Later, I was cocktailing at the Red Lion Inn in Vancouver Washington. One night, I was serving drinks at a table, and as I was collecting the money, I looked up. In the distance across the room, I saw Ray. I forgot about collecting the money and nearly dropped my tray of drinks. I just walked over to him. My heart stopped, and I was shocked to see that he was watching me.

He wanted to go home with me when I got off work. Wow, that would be great. Ray was back. But there was a problem; Mark the creep was back staying with me. Did I need to be with sick men or just to have a man in my bed? In order to fuck me, a man had to be a sick one and an asshole, a real bad boy.

I told Ray we could not go to my house because it wouldn't be fair to the kids. What a lame excuse. I told him I would go to his house, and the next night we would go to mine. I went to his place, but something was wrong. I did not feel he wanted me there. I know he wanted to go to my house to make sure I was not with anyone. Then he would be back.

What sickness made me have Mark back in my house? Why couldn't I just be by myself for a while, hoping Ray would come back, that it would just take some time?

No, I messed up again. I went home the next morning, and Ray was shut down again. He never let me back in. I know that he loves me and I will be the one he loves truly from the heart.

Years later, I got a call. When I picked up the phone, I heard "No Blue Thing" by Ray Lynch. Ray had bought the tape for me, and I loved it. I knew the call was from him. I called him, but he denied playing the song we both liked. Still, he was the only one who knew it was my favorite.

Ray said he was in a relationship and that his girlfriend was young and very jealous. He thought she was like a rosebud that would bloom into a good woman and then things would be good for them. I did not think so. She knew he loved me for real. I knew it, he knew it, and that was the way it was.

All those men and never have I felt again like I did with Ray. Only once did I know what it felt like to be in love. I will know when it is there again, and I hope to feel it again before I die. We can dream because without our dreams we have nothing.

LARRY NUMBER ONE AND THIRD HUSBAND: THE PHOTOGRAPHER WITH HIDDEN DEBT

I thought Larry was gay when I first met him.

I started going up to Government Camp every weekend for the snow and all my friends. I would try to ski, but I was the snowball coming down the mountain. I did wear the name-brands clothes, so I looked the part. I took group and private lessons, but nothing worked for me.

So I made a trip or two and held the table in the lodge for ten people. I had my Spanish coffees, and I was happy. I had a lot of friends.

One day, a friend of mine said he wanted me to meet his best friend. I wasn't sure about the suggestion because I thought he was gay and wondered what kind of friend he had. Still, I said okay.

The next weekend, his friend was with him. Larry Watson was average-looking, but he had a good personality and was very nice to talk to. He looked gay too.

Larry asked me out, and we started dating. The sex was so great that, again, I thought it must be love. Isn't this the way you were supposed to feel through sex? I do not know why, but as you know, it was the only way I knew how to feel. I really didn't know better. I thought this was the way. Well, I didn't think. If only I had been thinking with my brain, rather than just with the cunt.

I always thought that, if the sex was good, everything was good and the man I was sleeping with must be nice too. So I'd settle in, and after I'd get to know the person, I usually would find I didn't like him. I would try to see if we were compatible, and in the end, we never were; we were nothing alike, and I didn't even like him. That was the pattern—good sex; it must be love; live with him or marry him; but who is this person? Isn't that the way it is done?

I did things backward. I had sex with a man and then got to know him, and then I ran. And after he was gone, I'd do it again. What a cold way to live. But the more sex and the more men I had the more I would feel; otherwise, I would feel empty.

Larry was a photographer. He traveled all over the states, including Alaska. I had sold my house on SE Sherman and had my furniture in storage. I was staying at my sister's.

Larry and I grew close, as was my pattern when sex was good. He asked me to marry him. Yes, of course, I agreed. He was fun, and sex was good. Kissing me all over, he could make me sweat. His cock was the right size. He could go down on me and make me scream and then shove that great cock in me. What a feeling. What else mattered? We should live happily ever after.

I moved into his place. He had a Porsche in the garage that he had leased. After a while, I could tell he could not afford the car. He was a big talker and a big spender. Had a nice house that I thought he'd bought from his boss. I told him he needed to give the car back to the rental company. He didn't want to—the Porsche gave him status I guess—but he did.

We planned a wedding. When we first started planning, it was great. I was paying for everything, and Larry kept saying he would pay me back. I had already been planning for a while, and the invites were out for the wedding date, and he still hadn't paid me. When I'd started to buy things for the wedding, I kept thinking that he would give me money when he got back from the job he was on. But no; the check he received from the company he worked for, Sorenson Photography, wasn't much. Instead, I started to charge everything. I had money, and, yes, I paid for the whole wedding

I knew Larry made a lot of money. I had seen the work orders. I could not understand what was going on. I started to go with him to work. I flew to Alaska after he drove there and got set up. He was taking portraits for a credit union.

We drove back. The mosquitoes were as big as birds. I thought they were going to eat me up. It was a fun trip. We saw big brown bears alongside the road, which was scary. As we were driving at night, the sky started to light up. The light got bigger and bigger like a big circle or a funnel going straight to earth from the sky. I got really scared until Larry explained that what we were looking at were the Northern Lights. I had heard of them in a song. But I had never seen them. To me, it seemed like Martians were coming to get us; I knew it. The display was so huge, and so many lights were shooting up and down and all around in a circle.

Larry pulled over so he could go to the bathroom. I told him he couldn't leave me here alone, and I was not getting out. When he got out, I locked the doors. When he got back, I told him that, if we come across a bar, I needed to pick me up a drink. He did not drink. We'd been on the road with so many miles of darkness and no cars, and we were targets for the aliens. This was so beautiful and scary.

Out of the dark appeared a bar. We got a Baileys to calm me down. The bartender also assured me that I was safe and that I should enjoy the lights.

We got back home, and Larry got his paycheck. It was not enough to cover the bills. I decided it was time for me to get involved. I gathered and totaled all the receipts from our trip and had Larry turn them in to his boss, as he should have been doing all along. I explained that he and his boss, Bill, should be taking all the expenses off the total they received for the shoot and then splitting the net. Rather, all of the expenses had been coming out of Larry's split.

We got a new paycheck, but Bill was not happy. He did not think this new arrangement—with me keeping tabs on the money coming in and going out—was going to work. Larry was just easygoing and happy to do the work. He didn't watch out for himself or manage his bill at all, and it was driving me nuts.

After Bill decided he wasn't happy with the accounting change, Larry started on his own. I acted as his partner, doing the work after the shoots out of the house. This included having the film developed and shipped and collecting the money owed.

One day, a visitor knocked at the door and handed me a paper. It was Bill, Larry's former boss; the paper was a notice stating that, if the down payment for the house was not paid in thirty days, the house would go back to Bill Sorenson.

You see, Larry had had the house for two years and had never given Bill the two thousand-dollar down payment. I went to an attorney and asked what I should do. Following the lawyer's advice, I got a two thousand-dollar money order off my credit card and sent the papers to Bill.

Now not only had I paid for the wedding, I had paid the down payment he still owed on the house. And once, before we got married, I had driven my car to Idaho to be with Larry through snow and ice all the way. When I got there and we started looking at wedding things and making plans, I broke out in hives. Yes, the sign that I shouldn't be planning on getting married had come back. What more of a sign does one need? I only broke out in hives when I talked about or looked for wedding items.

I thought that Larry made good money. He had once flown me to Idaho to be with him while he worked. He'd had me put the airfare on my visa, promising to pay me back. That was the first of many times he'd do something like that and then fail to come up with the money. Now do you see red flags?

I think that someone who was in her right mind might have seen very clearly that something was wrong with this picture. Well, as we know, Larry never got his full paycheck. But he never took care of his bills either. When I moved in, I discovered that the third bedroom was full of receipts; he had boxes full of them. I hired my daughter to help me sort them by dates and years. When we were done, I took them to an accountant. He said Larry owed so much in back taxes that he could go to jail.

By this time, I had had enough, and I filed for a divorce. I talked to Larry about it, and so that he would not get the house taken away from him, I had him sign the house over to me. That is when I paid the two thousand dollars he owed on the house and gave Larry the divorce papers. He knew I was having a girlfriend serve him the papers, and he was fine with this.

We stayed friends, but I paid for the half I owed from the marriage, and collectors kept coming to the house looking for him because he never paid his half of the bills. They bugged me because they did not know how to find him; they only had my address. What a mess.

CHAPTER EIGHT

LAKE OSWEGO: MY THIRD HOUSE

BARRY: HE LIKED ME; HE JUST LIKED YOUNGER GIRLS BETTER

BARRY OWNED A BUILDING IN downtown Portland, where he hosted comedy acts. The place had a nice bar and restaurant. We met and enjoyed getting together for sex. He was always nice, and the sex was good; he did aim to please.

Barry liked girls who were very young, so we never did date. We never were long-term sex partners. He was okay but not that great in bed for me. We stayed friends over time.

Barry had never been married, though he did have two kids with a very young partner who liked to drink and maybe do drugs.

He was nice-looking and wealthy. And he was nice to see once in a while.

TED: STOLE MY ID

I met a guy named Ted when I was out with some friends. He asked me out, and I thought, *Why not.* So we got together.

Ted said he ran a top construction company. But he lived in a small camp trailer with his son. Something was wrong with this picture.

I had a very nice home in Lake Oswego and had done some remodeling, and he started telling people that he had done the work. In addition, I learned that his son, who was in high school, had no money for school clothes. So I bought him some clothes. I soon realized that I needed to get out of this situation. Yes, the sex was good, but the rest wasn't.

I told Ted I could not see him anymore.

One night he said he had to talk to me. When I agreed, he gave me a diamond ring.

I said, "I do not want this."

He screamed and said he wanted me and wanted me to wear the ring.

I pretended to throw the ring and left his place and went home.

A month later, I got a call from a collector saying that I needed to pay for the ring, as I hadn't been making the payments. I assured the caller that I had never opened an account with his store. The guy said he had a feeling that this was what happened. I asked how the account could have been opened in my name in the first place, and he explained that Ted had opened it and had provided my driver's license number and address. The store owner said he would mail something for me to sign and have notarized. After I had sent it back, he would take care of the situation so that I would not have to deal with it. He would go after Ted for them money. I gave him whatever information I had on Ted.

At one point, my daughter and I had to call the school Ted's son attended to ask the son to tell Ted to leave me alone. It had gotten bad.

STAN NUMBER TWO: TOOK MY BREATH AWAY FOR TEN YEARS

I went into a bar in Beaverton called Bebop's. The place was always busy, and all my girlfriends and I were there three times a week. That's where I met Stan, who was tall and good-looking. I fell for him the instant I saw him. We talked and danced and he asked me if we could get together.

Stan was a banker; he was not only very classy, he was just plain sexy. He had a smile that would light up the room, black hair, and brown eyes.

I invited him to my place. We connected like fire, hot fire. But he would never date me. He'd just call now and then. And every time he did, we just went for it hot and heavy.

I desired him for ten years or more. He was so beautiful. I could not figure out why not me. He told me one time that, if he dated me, he would end it, and that would be it. He could not commit. Boy, did I know that one. We got together two times a year. I always loved these times; I loved to look at him and be in bed with him naked. This man fit the dream I'd always had. He was so good-looking, tall, and beautiful, and it felt so right. We made a good-looking couple indeed.

I liked him so much that I let him come over to my house knowing I was pregnant and having an abortion in a few days. He did come over, but he didn't know what was going on with me. And I just wanted to be with him.

He did get married eventually, to the daughter of the family who owned Rheinlander restaurant on Sandy Boulevard—yes, someone with a name of substance. But he came to me, saying he was very unhappy and wanted to see me. He wanted to know if that was okay, so he could make it in his marriage.

I said, "*No*, that does not work for me. When and if you get a divorce, call me."

He said that he would be ending things with his wife and that he would call. He did, and yes, we got together again. I was living on my floating home at this time. He would call, and before he'd get in the door, we would have our clothes off. It was so hot, hot, hot. We would do it on the stairs, in the entryway, wherever.

One thing about Stan was that he would not spend the night; it was like making a commitment.

One day, he called and said he really wanted to see me. We started talking, and he said that he wanted to have a baby with me and marry me. He was going to France, and he wanted me to think about this proposal while he was away. He said that he really cared about me and he knew that being with me was what he really wanted.

He really wanted me. After ten years, Stan was saying this to me. All I could think about was that this was really, finally happening. I did not want another child, but with Stan, I felt differently. I would have loved to have his baby.

He sent me a postcard from France saying that he was having fun there. When he got back, he could not wait to see me and tell me about all his adventures. I had the fireplace going and a bottle of wine open. We made passionate love. I could not wait to talk about what he'd said before he left. He wanted me forever—that was all that was on my mind.

We were lying in front of the fireplace and just enjoying what we'd shared. He started talking about how happy he was with his life and knowing what he wanted and how he knew that he had fallen in love. I was feeling very happy too. And I was so excited that my Stan was here with me saying all this.

Then he finished with, "Marilyn, I just have to tell you again that I am so in love and know what I want for the first time." And then he explained that he had met this girl in France and was going back there to ask her to marry him.

I just dropped to the floor. I don't think he knew how I had taken what he had been saying or how what he'd just said had hit me. I listened and simply said that it was late and maybe we should call it a night.

Why was I being so nice again? My whole world had just blown up in my face and I had just been used again for my body, for sex. He had given no thought to my heart. I was so hurt. I just cried after he left.

He never married the girl in France. She did not feel the same way, and it was a whim to him.

One day, I was reading *the Oregonian*, and I turned to the obituaries, a section I never look at. I just glanced, and there was Stan. He had died at forty-eight years old. I was shocked. He had gotten married after all. And then two years later, he got sick and died. I thought about going to the funeral, but I didn't. I never forgot him.

ALAN: FOURTH AND LAST HUSBAND, SEPTEMBER 1990–1992

During my days of going to Bebop's, I was sitting at the bar talking to the bartender. She and I were best friends, and she was kind of possessive of our friendship. She asked if I would like a Spanish coffee; the man at the other end of the bar wanted to buy it for me. I said, "No."

Linda said, "He's a nice guy." She told me he'd been coming into the bar for a year. "Why not have a drink?" she added.

So I did. His name was Alan. After I said thank you, we started to talk. He seemed nice. He was okay-looking, nothing to write home about.

Alan asked me out. We would go to dinner or meet for a drink. You know what happens next. My clit started doing the thinking; we had to have sex of course. What else was dating about? I didn't consider dating for a while without sex—something healthy like maybe getting to know him. Really when it came down to it, it was about the sex first, right? Then you'd get to know the guy.

I would eventually get it right later in years, after all those cocks, cocks, and more cocks. Come, come, come—that was how I thought you got to know a person. And of course, I figured that a man must really care if he took me to bed. Wow, we loved each other now.

I didn't know that, one day, I would wake up and know the real way to feel. For now, sex equaled love, and that was the way it was.

One thing led to another, and after we'd gone out for a few months, Alan moved in with me. Alan lived in an apartment, and I lived in my beautiful home in Lake Oswego. I was remodeling it. He was a plumber and could do many of the remolding needs himself, so he took over remolding my house, using my money of course. He did great work, and so the work on my house was going well.

The sex—now we get to it—was out of this world, probably the best I have ever had, again (or at least one of the best)! When we kissed, my clothes would just fly off. His cock was the right size; as you know this was very important to me. I did not want to be shorted at all, or I'd throw him back. There were plenty of other cocks out there. His cock was about six inches long and plenty thick, and it fit in my mouth perfectly. He could go down on me, and I did not know anything else in this world existed when I had my multiple orgasms. He would put his cock in me, and the sensations would just explode all over my body.

Now that we were having great sex and we were living together, how would we get along? Alan drank way too much. When we are out, he would become rude, unfriendly, and obnoxious. Once we were out at Bebop's and I wanted to introduce him to a guy friend of mine who was a very good friend. Alan looked at me drunkenly and said, "Why would I want to meet that asshole?"

That is how it went. We would get in arguments, and I would just ignore him when he drank too much. Then when he was sober, I would have a talk with him, telling him how much the way he behaved when he was drunk bothered me.

One time, I just said, "This isn't working for me; enough is enough."

We were going to church together at the Living Enrichment

Center. I had been going to this church for a few years now. It was great. Alan stopped drinking for nine months. While he was sober, we had a good time with family and friends.

I usually took Wednesdays off, just to have a day in the week to get things done and to have me time. All of a sudden one day, Alan did not go to work. I asked why, and he said he was taking Wednesdays off. I was fuming inside. Why? Well, he needed a day off too, but not my day off. I needed this for myself. He was not happy, and neither was I.

Alan's folks came from Oklahoma to visit us. They had money and were not happy about us being together. They loved Alan's ex-wife, Pam. They just came to see what I was all about and why Alan had left his wife for me. They clearly thought I was the reason his marriage had ended.

What a story to tell. I did not know that Alan was married when we got together. His wife lived in Oklahoma. He was here on a large plumbing job.

We got married on September 30, 1990. We had met in April or May. It was a great wedding with a beautiful cake. The reception was at a place on the waterfront. The next day, we headed for Hawaii for our honeymoon. This was a disaster.

How had I come so far with this? I was following my pattern. When would I learn? Obviously not yet! We were out to dinner at one of the finest restaurants in Hawaii. The place was incredibly beautiful and classy. We sat for a while and ordered a drink or two. The waiter came back to take our order, and Alan made a smart remark. I asked him to try and watch what he said. "Let's have a nice evening," I told him.

The next thing I knew, he yelled something out—something about me wanting the guy next to us or the waiter; I don't remember the specifics. It was just so embarrassing.

I got up and left. I just wanted to go home.

In the days of my past, stress, yelling, arguments, or negativity, not to mention talking marriage, would cause me to break out in hives. Well, guess what? It wasn't hives now; it was my back. My back went out in Hawaii. This started to happen whenever there was any arguing or yelling. Searing pain would streak down my spine. This had happened with other boyfriends who like to argue as well. I would be in an argument on the phone, and I'd just have to hang up to keep my back from going out completely.

I always had something telling me when a situation wasn't right; if it wasn't hives, it was shooting pain in my back. And it would happen every time negative or unhealthy things were going on with boyfriends or dating. I was given the signs; I could have heeded the voice inside the hives and the back pain. Those signs hit me like a ton of bricks, pleading with me to listen. But I didn't listen, so I paid the painful price.

So how did I always get into my messes? I did not listen to the inner voice that guides us. What did I do instead? I just ignored it. You dummy. Wake up and listen. Oh not yet; I apparently needed more drama and hurt in my life.

When Alan's folks were at our place visiting, I woke up one morning and walked into the kitchen. They were talking about money and the five thousand dollars Alan was borrowing from them. I was shocked. I decided to let them know that I did not know anything about the money. I added that I had not known that Alan was married when we'd gotten together. I would not have dated him or married him if I had had any idea. That was not the kind of person I was. The money was Alan's thing; I did not know why he was borrowing because he was working.

Alan told me about his aunt who was worth a million or so and had no kids. He said he knew that, when she passed, he would not have to work at all. That in combination with his parents' wealth would ensure that he wouldn't have to work. I believe he just floated from job to job. He didn't want to work hard, so he didn't. Instead, he just borrowed from his parents.

In December we had been married for four months. Alan said he had to go to Oklahoma to see his parents and take care of some business. I thought nothing of this. What a shock I got. The day after he left, the mailman came as always, and I went to pick up the mail from the mailbox. In it was a letter for Alan that looked very important. I could not resist opening it. The letter contained divorce papers from his wife, Pam, in Oklahoma. They were not divorced, and guess where he was?

When he came back home, I pretended not to know what the letter was about. We had a long drawn-out talk, full of sadness, about how he could do this to me.

I was actually trying to get pregnant. Alan had never had a child and had been married for seventeen years. I had wanted another child. Having a baby together seemed like the thing to do. We even went to special-needs adopting classes. Sounds good, right?

Come on. Look at my story now with Alan. Where did my mind live, in fairy-tale land? Did I just not see any of the negativity or the big red flags?

We would collect his sperm and take it to the testing place near us. We had to hurry and get there in a certain amount of time. He had a low sperm count. I could get pregnant, but the chances were slim.

Around February, we went to church for a special event. The speaker took people on rafting trips, and he also traveled, speaking on relationships and how rafting could be analogous. As he spoke, I became engrossed in listening to what he was saying. His words were like a wake-up call for me.

When my first grandchild, Felicia, was born on December 29, 1990, something happened in my chest. Before her birth, I'd put up what felt like a concrete wall and had not felt anything with my heart. When Felicia was born, my chest became warm and my heart was filled with feelings. What was happening?

Now, something similar was happening six weeks later. As I

listened to the speaker named Charley, my whole being started feeling, and my life started making sense. I felt such a rush. I felt more of an understanding of what life was about, and I knew what the man sitting beside me was about.

I turned and looked at Alan and not just with my eyes; my whole body was open to who he was and who I was with him. I said to myself, *Listen.* What the speaker was saying was clearing things up for me about what our mates should be to us. He asked, does your mate respect you? Treat you with love? Wow, this man next to me was not good for me. The situation was not healthy. *This is him, I told myself. Alan is this person, not the person I should be with.*

Wow, I loved going to that church. I always saw the truth more clearly every time I went.

That day especially was such an eye-opener and the start of a change in my life.

Even though I could feel now the warmth from my chest, there have been times when I've wanted the concrete wall back on my chest. Now when I am hurt, I really feel it. I feel sometimes that I can't bear the hurt and wish I could just put the wall in my chest back up.

As for Alan, I knew then that I needed to part ways with him. I know you already figured this out—the sex was good. Even the sex I wanted less and less as his true self came out. I just cringed when he wanted to touch me. Now I knew I wanted to get out of this marriage. I wasn't sure, but I didn't think we were even legally married.

Again Alan had to go to Oklahoma; for what, I did not know. He said he had to get some things or something, but I felt he was not telling me the truth. When he'd moved in, he'd never unpacked his boxes; they were in storage under my house.

While Alan was gone, I called my girlfriend and asked her to help me. I changed the locks on the house and got a U-Haul truck and put everything of Alan's in the truck. How nice that his boxes were still packed. We rented a storage unit at the U-Haul place, emptied the truck, and left the key with the storage company. I called and left a message with Alan, explaining that all of his things were at U-Haul storage, that I had changed the locks on the door, and that I was filing for a divorce.

He called me crying. He wanted to make it work. He'd always wanted to have someone like me. He meant my looks, my body. He wasn't thinking of me as a person. His looks were average, and he was about five foot nine. He was slightly balding and had a stocky build and one of his eyes kind of looked in another direction. I never cared. He was good in bed and a bad boy. Was there anything else?

You must know you're going to follow me on another roller-coaster ride now.

I went to a divorce attorney and explained that I wanted an annulment. To my surprise, I could not get one. The fact that Alan was still married in another state did not matter here. "What?" I said. "This isn't right. He's married."

Apparently, he could be; our system is so screwed up. This is one example of how our government is a mess. I won't get into that subject, as it's another book entirely. Actually hundreds of books have already been written on that subject.

I asked the lawyer what I could do. He explained that I could get a divorce for four hundred dollars or I could try to go for an annulment but that would cost me a thousand, and he did not think that was the best way to go.

I filed, and Alan was served. He wanted the ring he'd paid for back; apparently he'd used part of his (and Pam's) savings to pay for it. He also wanted the lawn furniture and one other thing he'd bought. I said no to the latter two, though I did give the ring back. I shouldn't have after all he'd put me through. But it was over and done. What a whirlwind—or a storm more like it.

A few months after the divorce was final, Alan called just to talk. He told me he was going to Las Vegas and asked me to meet him there. At first, I said no. But he really wanted to see me. He said that we'd have fun and that I should just come, and he promised to be on his best behavior.

I thought, why not? It might be fun.

I got to Vegas on a Friday afternoon. We met and checked into our room. I do not know what happened, but suddenly, our clothes flew off and we were having the best, mad, passionate sex—not lovemaking, just downright nasty, hot, fucking, every way but loose. After a few hours, we went to the casino to have something to eat and to gamble a little. Before we knew it, we were back in the room going at it again for a few hours. We took another break and went and watched a Las Vegas show.

It was early in the morning when we went back to the room. I think we planned to sleep. We got undressed and got into bed, and there we were at it again. I was in heaven. Thank you, God. Thank you, God. We slept, and when we woke up, we were at it again. That is how the weekend went. Lots of great, great sex, over and over again.

We said our good-byes, and that was that. I told him that we would not get back together and thanked him and left.

I heard that he was back with his wife, Pam. I believe they were never divorced.

DAN: THE COUNTRY BOY WITH MONEY

I was at, you guessed it, Bebop's dancing and having a good time. Every time I went, I would see this tall, nice-looking guy. He seemed wholesome, so of course, I was not attracted to him. Still, he always talked to me.

One time, I was walking in front of the bar, and he picked me up and flipped me over his shoulders. I said okay; I would go out with him.

Dan was a very nice guy, so of course I was not attracted to him; he did not have a shadow of asshole. He had money, a nice home, and lots of cars, and his friends had money too. We had good fun. I stayed at his place once or twice, but that was all. The sex was good, just good; remember, he was a nice guy—the type I wasn't attracted to, so sex was just sex.

He asked me to go to a party his friends were having, and I said yes. All the partygoers were couples, and we had lots of fun.

At one point, Dan sat me down and said he had something to say. He explained that he had money and that, if I were with him, I would not have to work or want for anything. He wanted to marry me. He had never been married and had never proposed to anyone before.

I was shocked. I could not believe what I was hearing. You see, I had been asked to get married so many times, and no one knew me. The men who wanted me as their wife knew only my looks and that I was nice and fun. But no one knew me.

I told Dan that I did not know him and that I could not marry him. We would need to get to know one another better. The truth was I just wanted to go home. I should have taken his proposal as a compliment, but I didn't. I cried all the way home. I just wanted to find someone to be a friend to me and to have fun with, someone who did not want to marry me or confine me or have sex with me—a friend.

JOE: THE BIG GUY (YES, IT WAS BIG TOO!) AND MY LAKE OSWEGO HOME

Joe and I had sex once for nineteen hours straight. I met him through some friends, and we liked each other from the start. He was six foot one and had brown hair and eyes and a great build; he was all muscles.

We started dating a little, though mostly, we were having great sex. We had sex everywhere you can imagine.

My home in Lake Oswego was on the side of a hill, and I was moving dirt out from under the house to make a master bedroom and bath and a giant entryway. Joe helped dig and haul dirt out with my son. That was nice of him, and the rewards were plenty.

The thing I remember most about Joe was that nineteen-hour fucking marathon. I was at his house, and we started in the afternoon and fucked and fucked every way but loose. We would take a shower, and would pick me up and hold my pussy to the shower head to rinse or soak it, as I was getting sore. Then we'd be back to fucking only to return to the shower. We did go to the kitchen and eat whatever we could—mostly doughnuts for energy.

We got together like this for three months. I stopped because, one day, we were at his house, of course having wild, wild sex, and the phone rang. Joe answered. It was his mom. He was having a good conversation with her, and all of a sudden, I heard, "No, Mom, I'm just working and keeping to myself." He explained that he hadn't gotten over his ex.

I thought, *Who am I then?* Hearing him say he had no one in his life made me feel empty again. After three months of us spending time together, his mom was thinking, *Poor Joe, he's just staying home sad.*

His mom sent the doughnuts we were eating, and she was going to send another care package.

BIRNEY: ENGLISH SOCCER PLAYER

I was at Bebop's with some girlfriends, and this cute, sexy English guy started talking to me. He was a soccer player. He asked me out, and I said yes.

Birney was so cute and fun, and having sex with him was so much fun. It seemed that every time we went out, we took my Porsche, and his billfold was always in the glove compartment.

We went to a New Year's Eve dance at the Last Laugh in downtown Portland, and we parked and got to the door to buy tickets, and he had no billfold. Yes, he was very cheap. This happened over and over.

Birney did like going out and meeting young girls once a week. He said there was nothing to it, just talk. He was going to meet a certain girl again the second or third time. I did not like it. He said I was number one and took me to all the important events. I knew that he was going the Dublin Pub in Beaverton, as he went there on Wednesday nights. So I got three of my girlfriends, and we all put on our short, leather skirts and headed to the Dublin.

All four of us girls walked in standing tall and strutting our stuff; we all looked hot. Barney was sitting at the bar and, yes, talking to the young blond girl I knew he was meeting. We walked by him, and he just about shit; if you could see the look in his eyes. We just kept walking, went to a table, and sat down.

Birney came right over to our table and straight to me. He started talking and saying he did not know what to do. He asked if I wanted him to sit with me or what?

I said, "No, sit with your friend."

He was so nervous.

What do men think—that we just sit and wait for them, as if we have no brains or feelings?

This was not good. What did he think he was doing? He needed a lesson, and I needed to put him in his place. Doing so felt so good.

Birney did ask me to meet with his psychologist and tell him what I thought of him. He respected me and knew I saw things as they were. I did have lunch with his therapist. Everything I said about Birney he already knew. Birney was self-centered and into himself, but he was trying to better himself, and I guess he had come a long way. I wouldn't have liked seeing him before.

I had a great house with white carpet and a dog named Sammy. I just got a little puppy, a long-haired Doxy I named Maxwell. One day, Birney was coming by to pick me up for a date. He walked in, and he did not even look at the cute, little puppy, not to mention ask about him. I knew then that Birney did not have a heart. In my opinion, any person who doesn't like animals is heartless.

Soon after the incident with the blond, I wanted to move on, and I did. A month or two later, I found out that I was pregnant. I was shocked. I did not tell Birney. He did not want any more kids. I did, but not his. I had just had a colonoscopy, so the fetus could have been injured. I was sick. Both my daughter and daughter-in-law wanted to get pregnant, and here I was, pregnant.

I could not take a chance that something would be wrong with the baby, so I scheduled an appointment to have an abortion on Monday, March 19. On March 17, I went out with some girlfriends to Jake's Bar for a Saint Patty's Day party.

Everyone was there, including Birney. I did not tell him what was going on with me. My friends thought I should, but the choice was mine, and I did not want him to know about the pregnancy at all. He never did know.

Sometime down the road, he came into Bebop's looking for me. He knew I always went there, and he came over and sat by me. He asked if there was any chance that we could get back together.

I said never, and he was disappointed and surprised; his ego thought I would take him back.

José: Classy Man

I was at Bebop's with a bunch of girlfriends again; it was our Friday girls' night out. This guy came up to talk. He was nicely dressed; his suit was out of place in this bar. He looked classy, and he walked with pride. He was around five foot eight, not tall, and he was Spanish.

We started talking, and then we danced. José asked me out—surprise. We had some nice dates. He was very nice and mannerly. He adored me and wanted to commit to me right away.

I was not so attracted to him. Not surprisingly, the reason came down to sex. I did not like having sex with him. His dick was very long and skinny. It turned me off. At one point, he suggested that we could have anal sex. I told him that he must be kidding, explaining that I would never go there. He said that, if we had anal, I would not have to worry about getting pregnant. He explained that he and his ex had avoided pregnancy by having sex that way. Yuck; that was not me.

I did not have the heart to tell him that the problem was his dick—that it turned me off. I liked a nice dick and always wanted one of my own, with a man I was attached to.

José and I had only gotten together a few times when I received a package from UPS. Inside was a robe and toothbrush. I about shit my pants. No way did I ever want to see this man's dick or have sex with him again. I could not go down on him knowing he liked anal sex; besides, it was an ugly dick. I packaged the robe and toothbrush back up and sent it back to him with a note that explained that this did not work for me. I did not want a commitment from him. I just wanted to be friends; that was all.

Through the years, I would see José come into Bebop's and watch me, always with caring eyes. He would come up and say hi. I would just say hello and go about my business. I never invited him to sit with us.

Years later, he called. I was living on my houseboat, and I planned to attend a brunch on the waterfront that Sunday. The brunch was always a fun event to go to. I invited José to come.

When he showed up, he was much wider than I remembered. His weight gain turned me off. We visited, and it was nice seeing him, but now I was really not attracted to him. He said his sister or a friend was staying with him and cooking. He made a comment about how, if we were together, I would get him in shape. I said, "You better know it."

Twenty years later, I saw his son on an advertisement, and I called to say hi to his dad. José had moved back east and thought I would be happy there. He said I should think about coming to visit and living with him. He still wanted to be with me. I did not know if I should be flattered or just sad for him. He wanted someone, and like me, he still hadn't found anyone.

MIKE NUMBER FIVE:
SEX ANYWHERE WE COULD FIND

Mike and I had good sex; he could take care of my body. Was that what I lived for? I guess that was where my brain was. I lived at my mom's house in between homes.

What a little cutie Mike was. He was just a nice gentleman. He lived out of town, and we met at a gathering downtown at a bar. When we first started dating, he would come into town every other weekend. We would go out to dinner or to see a movie or for a drive. Since I was staying at my mom's house and his home was out of town two hours away, we would go to the park and have sex on the grass or sometimes in his car. Now and then, we rented a room.

I always enjoyed Mike, but the relationship wasn't going anywhere. We lived too far apart, and neither of us was going to move. The sex, wherever it took place, was getting to be too much.

CHAPTER NINE

MY FLOATING HOME ON HAYDEN ISLAND

JOHN NUMBER ONE (DON): BAD NEWS (THE KIND OF MAN WHO MAKES YOU REALIZE YOU REALLY SHOULD LISTEN TO YOUR INNER VOICE)

I WAS OUT WITH THE GIRLS, this time at the Greenwood Inn. My girlfriend was flirting with some guy she wanted to meet. I could care less. I was not attracted to the guy, so I was trying to help her meet him. I went up to him and asked him to come over to the table. He did, and he and my girlfriend met. He was acting more like he wanted to talk to me, so I ignored him.

The next time I saw him, the girls and I were at Bebop's sitting at the bar and he walked by. I was talking with another guy, and he was asking me out. I told him I'd had a date once. Why would I want another?

Just then, Don stopped to talk. "Look out," the guy I was talking to warned. "She will shoot you down."

Don did ask me out. All the girls kept saying that I should go out with him. Against my better judgment, I did. And another story began.

Don and I hit it off. I was still living in my great house in Lake Oswego, and he was living with his mom and had no job. He had a sweet little son. Don had a full head of nice white hair; one of his eyebrows was black and the other one was white. He was not working at the time, but when he did, he was an iron worker. He had nice parents and a good family. He was fun and liked to do things. He was just average but nice and poor.

He was good in bed, and I had orgasms. That was my brain. Who said just guys think with their other heads? I'm proof that some women think with their clits. That is obvious throughout this book. Was I nuts? With Don, I ignored so many red flags, and I continued seeing him even though I didn't feel right about it from the beginning. Yes, I moved him in.

I loved my home, but one day, Don and I were walking on some docks with floating homes. We started looking at the homes. I had always wanted one. I found one that day, and we talked to the Realtor about it. I wanted it.

Oh how my life was about to change—and not for the good; little did I know. I went home, and within three days, I had sold my beautiful house.

I bought the floating home, just like that. I had a garage sale. I wanted all new furniture that would be a good fit for a floating home.

I couldn't believe that I was selling my beautiful home in Lake Oswego. But I was excited. I had always wanted a floating home, and I had always wanted to live on the water. What an adventure.

Since Don was living with me, I decided to put him on the floating home insurance. I got a call from the insurance agent. The agent told me that he could not put Don on the policy, as Don had too many incidents on his record. He warned me not to get involved with this man, pointing out that Don's record did not look good and the he may well end up taking me. Big red flag!

Despite the warning and the fact that Don had no money, I still let him live with me; we were boyfriend and girlfriend. Come on, I was having sex. Isn't that what a relationship is about?

The night before I got the key, I had a barge waiting to start building a big, L-shaped deck, fifteen feet wide by forty-five feet by fifty-five feet. The work was completed in two days. What a dream.

We started working on my house.

I completely remodeled the place. I stripped out all of the carpet and repainted every room. The place had two big bedrooms, and the master bedroom had a bathroom the size of a bedroom with a sauna and a Jacuzzi. I actually hired some workers, and Don did a few things toward the remodeling. I took out several large, floor-to-ceiling windows from downstairs and replaced them with a sliding glass door. In the master bedroom, I had the carpenter install three windows and a sliding glass door that led to the deck. I found out how to paint tile and painted the bathroom tiles a shiny black. It worked.

For the final touches, I redid the kitchen counters with tile and put down new vinyl flooring. Throughout the rest of the house, I put in all new carpet.

On a floating home, you need good stringers and floats under the house, so I had a diver come check it all out. He dived in and looked under the house; we needed more foam. We also needed to have the home leveled so that I could have lots of people in the home at the same time.

When the diver and I met, we had an instant connection—a sexual connection. We just had to have each other, so we did. His kissing was great. When he got his cock out, oh Lord, it was so big that I wasn't even sure I wanted it in me. We tried, and it worked somewhat. Once was enough for me. He was incredibly sexy, but his cock was too big, wide, and weird-shaped. Yuck

We had to call the diver another time. A grocery cart filed with expensive tools fell in the river. The diver came back and got all the tools. We flirted, and he left. I knew what his cock was like, and I did not want to go there.

My home was good place for gatherings. I had Christmas parties, one for the adults and one for adults and kids. The Christmas boats came right in front of my deck. During the summers, I had barbecues for the family every Sunday, and on Sunday evenings, the adults sat on the deck and had margaritas.

I experienced so many disasters while living at the floating house. I was being sued by an ex-boyfriend and escaped attempted rape twice. In 1996, during the ice storm, the state told Hayden Island residents to evacuate because the water was rising.

The water got as high as two feet from the top of the piling. Most of us left the island, though some stayed. When we got back, we were hit with a windstorm. I thought that my houseboat was safely secured to the docks with good chains. All of a sudden, one chain broke (or so I thought). Rescuers came and took me and my two little doggies off of my deck. As soon as they did, the other chain broke.

It turned out that it wasn't the chains after all; they were good. The logs were old, and the wind kept them rubbing together until the wood just snapped. I had already called and gotten on a list to have a tugboat get my houseboat. The house went into the next dock, and two tugboats pulled it back in. The rescuers secured it until they could move me back to my space. What a ride.

Before that, the ice was wrapped around us, and it was so thick you could walk on it.

In addition, I had a pipe break. I got the leak stopped and turned off the water until someone could come and fix it. I had scheduled a party for that night, and even though the electricity was out, we still had the party. A friend worked on the pole and fixed it so we had temporary lights. Everyone came, and we had so much fun.

One thing led to another. I had a steam room in the master bath with a Jacuzzi for four people. One night, Don's son was staying the night. Don thought the two of them would get into the Jacuzzi. Don and I had never been in the Jacuzzi together, but he was going in there with his son. No, I did not think so. I caught Don and told him that there would be no days like that. I suggested that, if he asked his girlfriend to take a sauna or Jacuzzi with him, he might have a better relationship. I also told him that there was something perverted about him always asking his son to do things and not his girlfriend.

For Christmas, I bought Don a thirty-one-foot Trojan with the stipulation that he had to make the payments. Wasn't I just a nice girlfriend? All his friends thought so too. One day, he said he wanted to take his son up the river in the boat for a campout, just the two of them.

Something about his story felt wrong again. He left on a Friday and planned to come home on Sunday night. I called his ex and asked if Don had picked up his son. He hadn't.

When Don got home Sunday night, he walked in oh so happy and wanted to kiss me.

"Are you kidding?" I said. "Don't even touch me." I asked him who he'd been with and where.

He said that he had gone out by himself.

Too many things never felt right, and I questioned what was going on with Don all the time. I paid for the house, and he paid for groceries. Once, I was going to the store, and he gave me a check. When I got to the counter, I discovered that he had not signed the check. Boy, was I naive. I paid for the groceries.

The way things had gone down would come back to haunt me. We had to part ways, and when he left, he went to his mom's I guess.

I got a call from my attorney a week later. He asked me to come in to see him. When I got to his office, he started to go over what looked like divorce papers. I was shocked. My attorney said that it would have been better if I'd married Don. I had cohabitated monies. I was naive, nice, and stupid; I just keep doing this over and over.

We went to court, and right away, the judge did not like me. I wore a business suit, and Don wore sweats. His appearance said, "Poor me." My attorney said I needed to dress down.

Once we started with court, I found out that Don had sued two other women in the past. He kept me wrapped up in court for two and a half years; he had a very conniving attorney. He was known around the courthouse as an ambulance chaser. Don and his attorney would set me up by pulling stunts like making appointments for 9:00 a.m. and canceling them at 5:00 p.m. the night before we were to meet. My attorney and I would not know about the cancellation until we got to court the next morning, and it would cost me $150 for the hour. This happened over and over again.

In the end, the judge ordered me to give Don the Trojan and keep making the payments. I could not believe what I was hearing. The judge said, "Give it to him or go to jail."

Don took the boat. He moored it up the river. I hired someone to go get it late one evening, and we chained it to my dock.

This man, who was not working, had lived in my home and thought what was mine was his. In the beginning of our relationship, I had taken $18,000 out of my savings and put it in a checking account, to which I'd added Don's name. I'd kept that account open for three months and then closed it when I realized that the arrangement wasn't working like I'd thought it was. What was I thinking? Of course, I wasn't.

The judge ordered me to give Don half of what was originally in the account—$18,000. I could not show the court that the money had come out of my other account. I paid cash for everything and would give Don cash or sometimes a check. He'd put the money in his bank account and then pay the bill with his check, so it looked like he was paying for things, even though he had no job. Who was the stupid one? Not him.

I did get a restraining order that forbade him from coming near my floating home. He did. Our split and all that came with it was a mess that lasted for two and a half years. Don knew all the tricks.

I had just wanted to share; when we'd first met, I had thought, *poor Don*. Now I really knew what "poor Don" meant. He got 60 percent of my assets.

I thought of appealing the court's decision, but my attorney told me I would end up paying another $20,000 in court costs and I would lose. He pulled a file from a drawer and told me that it contained the paperwork from a case just like mine; the case had cost the person $20,000 and he or she had lost. Even though I had a good case and should have won, I had a bad judge.

In the end, I didn't appeal and decided to move on and not look back. But I left the office that day bawling. I could not believe our legal system.

I hired someone to break Don's legs. When the person I was hiring wanted all the money up front, I canceled the job. I did talk to a couple of guys who taught me what a hit man is. I just wanted Don's legs broken. But these guys would kill and bury a person. They even told me how they'd do it. They explained that we would talk about it once, and when we walked away from that meeting, they would act like the discussion had never occurred. I canceled that as well. I had nightmares. I wanted Don to pay, but I didn't want him dead.

Karma would get him. I just wanted to live long enough to see it come back to him.

Eventually, Fritz, who you will meet soon, moved me off the floating home into a home close to his. I ended up renting out my floating home. I thought that, given the three disasters—the ice storm, the wind storm, and an attempted rape—I needed to take a break. The man who rented my house ended up buying it.

STEVE: SECRETLY USED MY PLACE FOR DRUGS

I used to also go into the Harbor Side, a place on the waterfront. What a fun place. Everyone would go in there. My girlfriends and I went at least once a week, usually on Fridays. It was like home week—one big party full of friends.

During this time, I had a hot body and thought life was all about sex. I got the attention I was looking for. Of course, I was so stupid. I thought that if I got a man's attention that meant he liked me. Yes, those men wanted to do me. But did they want to date me? That was the question. Years later, I would figure out the difference.

My girlfriend introduced me to this younger guy she knew named Steve. Steve and I started talking, and it was so much fun. He asked me out, and I said yes. We would do things with my friends, like go to the waterfront.

He started staying at my place. I never did see his place. He was great in bed, which is how I judged whether or not I wanted to date a guy. If a guy could give me an orgasm, I thought that meant he cared for me. Again, what was I thinking?

I had parties on my floating home, and Steve would invite friends. Sometimes, he would make an excuse to leave, which I never understood.

One day, a friend of mine who also lived in a floating home asked me for a private conversation, saying that no one was to know that we had talked. This friend told me that Steve was using my place to sell drugs, specifically coke. I was in shock and insulted; I had been taken once again. My friend told me about the times Steve had been selling, and I remembered all the times he'd had to leave or meet with someone here and I'd thought his behavior was unusual. I dropped Steve and felt sick inside again. I was thankful to my friend for confiding in me.

FRITZ AND MY FIRST PASSPORT: LIFE IN A BEAUTIFUL, MILLION-DOLLAR HOME

Back when I was still living in my floating home, my daughter thought she had the perfect man for me to meet. She arranged for us to meet at a dance bar close to Gresham called the Flower Drum.

My daughter knew lots of people at the bar, but the friend who she wanted me to meet never showed up. I was stood up. Still, I had fun.

Fritz called and said he still wanted to meet at another time. I was not enthused. However, I agreed to meet him. He came over to Hayden Island with his son, and we met for a drink. He asked if we could get together again, and we did. His wife had just passed in December, and we met in February. He was looking for a girlfriend.

I was not attracted to Fritz. He was worn-looking and rough around the edges. And he was just a basic lover, if he could get it up. But I found him interesting, and we started to date. He invited me for a drive up around Corbett, a small town where I'd grown up. He had friends up there, and we went out for lunch at a tavern. We talked and found that we shared a similar upbringing and had been to a lot of the same areas in our pasts.

I sold my floating home, and, as you know, Fritz helped me move into a house that was close to his. My son moved in with me. We thought the house was haunted.

After my son met a great gal and the two of them moved in together, I moved in with Fritz. He had a big, beautiful home on some acres with a stream off of Foster Road. I had a lot of nice furniture, so I sold some from his garage. We put my big, black sectional in his living room. His kids made fun of it and gave me a hard time because I was there. Actually, his daughters didn't; they liked me. His stepdaughters and son gave me a bad time. Fritz didn't treat his daughters right.

Fritz's son was rude, and he and his wife both thought they were "it." Fritz treated his son and his grandson super well. He more or less ignored his two daughters, and they would talk to me about this situation. The stepdaughters, who were pretty and thin, unlike Fritz's own daughters, got all the attention. His daughters were nice as can be, but they weren't thin. The difference in the way Fritz treated the girls was very obvious, and it was difficult to watch.

I thought I wanted to clean the house and cook myself, rather than having the lady who lived on the property keep doing it. It was too much for me, but Fritz made me keep doing it. He said that I had wanted to do it, and now I should follow through. I couldn't keep up. I am not a cook.

Fritz's birthday was on July 4. Every year, the family celebrated with a big barbecue on the huge patio. I was told that everyone would do his or her part putting the food together. Someone had to talk with the guests and make sure everyone was being taken care of, and Fritz passed out somewhere for a while, so I talked and visited with everyone. I hosted as I should.

When the party was over, we were cleaning up and I could not find my two doggies anywhere. I looked everywhere. Fritz asked his son to help look, and we asked everyone who was around. No one had seen them. I kept looking.

I heard a sound from the back of the pickup into which everyone was throwing garbage. My babies had been put in the garbage in the back of the pickup. I knew this was Fritz's son's doing. He and his wife had liked me at first, but things had changed when their son starting preferring me over Fritz. Fritz's son and his wife wanted to brownnose Fritz, and that meant they wanted their little boy to go straight to Fritz when the family came over to visit. But when they walked in the front door, the little guy would look around the corner to find me; we would smile at each other, and he would run to me, not Fritz. Fritz's kids were always trying to get in good with him, and his son and his wife had thought they were on the top of the list and would get most of what he owned.

Fritz's stepsons treated me well, and one of his stepdaughters apologized for being rude and said she wanted us to be friends. That was nice. The other stepdaughter, who was Fritz's favorite, was very pretty, fiery, and spoiled. She had a daughter, and when they came over, the little girl always came up to me and gave me a big hug. Fritz was a growly, rough-looking man with a pockmarked face that looked like someone had smashed it.

Fritz said nothing to his son about what he had done to my dogs. Things like this kept happening. Fritz was not a lover. I did always try to please him, and I took care of his cock. I know I was too much for him, but I wanted a home, and I was trying. He always made sure the help would bring me all the firewood I needed to keep a fire going in the fireplace. I loved having a fire; it was so homey.

Fritz and I were talking one evening, and he walked over to the fireplace. His arms hung at his side, and his hands balled into fists. He said that he could not be what I needed. I knew that he meant sexually.

I told him that all I asked was that we make a home and be happy. I sexually intimidated him, and he did not know how to be a real lover.

Fritz sold some property and got a trip to Antigua out of the deal. So we went on vacation. I got a girlfriend of mine to stay at the house and watch my doggies while we were away. After what Fritz's son had done, I didn't trust anyone around my little doggies. I loved them so much.

While we were in Antigua, Fritz and I toured and had great dinners. I tried to please Fritz sexually, but he was just frustrated. I did not know why.

Then we were at an outside bar, having a drink and talking to other people about our travel plans. It sounded like so much fun. Then Fritz turned to me and said that he was not planning on taking me with him. I did not understand.

When we got home, Fritz said I had to move. His son and his

favorite stepdaughter would not come over anymore if I was there. This was the first of December. I had nowhere to go. I had $10,000 that I'd kept in his safe after selling my boat. He would not give it to me. He said it was his now. I told him I needed something so that I could get a place. He gave me a thousand dollars and said that was it.

My mom's sister had passed away just a few days before Fritz asked me to move out, and it was Christmas time. I had no money and no job. I had gotten rid of everything. How could someone treat a person the way Fritz was treating me? He had asked me to move in with him, and now he was treating me like I was completely unimportant.

I got a storage unit and a U-Haul truck. We waved and I drove off.

While I was with Fritz, I had been in court many times, dealing with Don's lawsuit and attempts to claim half of my assets as his own. Every time we had gone to court, Fritz had had his attorney sit with us. Between my attorney's fee of $150 an hour and his attorney's $150 an hour, the cost was $300 for every court appearance. When I left, Fritz was supposed to pay my attorney out of the money I had left in his safe. He did not and felt he did not have to, even though he had said he would.

I would hear that his daughters and stepdaughters would go out looking for me and report back to him about what I was doing. I wanted them to go away and leave me alone.

KEN: LIVED ON A FLOATING HOME

I met Ken walking around on the docks at the moorage near my houseboat. He did maintenance on the island. We became friends. We would hang out or have a drink together or go with our dates dancing at Red Lion. I would have family over for a barbecue, and he would bring his girlfriend over. She was very pretty and had long blond hair. I really liked hanging out with him.

One time when we were out, we saw Don's pickup truck. I had a restraining order against Don at the time. Ken went over and peed in his window inside the truck. He offered to do more, but I declined.

Ken was having a party at his floating home, and I went to visit and to meet his friends. He was drinking more than he normally did. People were leaving, and I wanted to go too. Ken just kept telling me to stay so we could talk. Soon, everyone had left except for one friend of his.

Ken started to touch me, and I said no. At first I thought he was just playing, but then he became aggressive. His friend said, "Leave her alone, and let her go home."

Ken grabbed me and pushed me down. He said he wanted me and kept saying, "Why not me? Let's do it." He was hurting me and holding me down and trying to rape me.

Ken's friend pulled him off me, and I ran out the door and ran home. I was so scared and shaken. My clothes were torn. I had been betrayed by my close friend. I would never talk to him again.

SECOND ATTEMPTED RAPE

I lived at the end of the dock, and the end of a row of seven floating homes. One night, I was out to dinner with Fritz; he worked at night, and it was his lunchtime. It was around 11:00 p.m. when I got back home and parked my car in the parking lot above the floating homes. I was walking toward the stairs that headed down to my dock when I noticed someone standing in the shadows. I kept walking.

Suddenly, the person came out of the shadows and said, "Hi, Marilyn. How are you doing?"

He scared me, and I felt something was wrong. It was a seventeen-year-old kid who lived three houses up from the dock. He kept walking with me and talking, seeming to want to make conversation. I just wanted to get home.

We got to the dock in front of his house, and he grabbed my arm and told me to come in. I told him no; I wanted to go home.

He pulled me, and I screamed, but no one seemed to have heard me. In his struggle to get me inside, he pulled me off the dock, and I slipped into the water, hurting my foot. He pulled me out and dragged me into his house. I could not stand on my foot. He attempted to rape me.

Then the phone rang. I was shocked when he went to answer it. His mom was calling, and he motioned for me to be quiet. I got up and ran out the door, calling the neighbors to come help me. I called Fritz, and the fire department came. Two men carried me up in a chair to the ambulance and took me to the hospital. I had to get a tetanus shot.

I guess the kid did drugs and was in trouble all the time. My neighbors said that they heard the screaming but they heard screaming from that house all the time and let it go, not knowing it was me.

I filed a complaint with the police, and they came to my house to take the report. I got an order preventing the boy from being on the same dock where I lived, and he had to go and live with his dad. The mother said that I had asked for it, that I'd wanted him. No wonder the kid had problems; his mom did not know how to handle him and was helping him get away with what he'd done to me.

We went to court, and I just made sure he would not be anywhere in the area.

BILL: YOUNG AND GOOD-LOOKING AND WANTED ME TO TEACH HIM ALL THE WAYS TO PLEASE A WOMAN!

I was at The Pilsner Room bar on the waterfront again with all my friends. This had become a two nights a week thing—an empty life. I had never seemed to figure out how to fill my time the right way. Anyway, I was sitting at the bar on a stool; I seemed to like to do that. A friend of mine came over to me and introduced me to a young man, who was nice-looking and seemed nice. My friend, Jeff, who since passed away at age sixty, told me that this young man wanted to meet me and would really like to take me out on a date.

Bill and I started talking, and we exchanged phone numbers. He called, and we did go out. He took me to a Blazers' game. He was twenty-five years younger than me.

I went out with him again, and this time, we had sex. He told me that he really wanted me to teach him all that I knew about making love to a woman. That was why he wanted to see me. He wanted me to teach him the ways of lovemaking and sexual pleasures. I did not.

He got married a few years later, and we always had special thoughts. I ran into him once when I was with Fritz at a car race that Fritz's brother was racing in. In the short moment that we could talk, Bill told me that his mom was Fritz's sister and that Fritz had raped her when she was a teenager. I was sick and hurried back to sit with Fritz so that he would not know we were talking. What was going on with my choices when it came to men?

CHAPTER TEN

MY CABIN IN THE WOODS

I N 1997, I BOUGHT MY home on the Willamette River. I called it my cabin in the woods. I owned a third acre with a sandy beach, and I didn't have an ounce of body fat, thanks to all the work I was doing to put my home together. I had a dozen trees cut down and hired some Hispanic workers through a friend to tear off the roof of the house. I rented a U-Haul truck, and a girlfriend and I picked up the shingles and took them to the dump.

My son, who can fix and build anything, built my deck, which extended out from the front of my cabin with a view of the river.

For three months, I did almost nothing but work on putting my home together. I was burning off everything I ate. At one point, I decided that I needed a break. I just wanted to go to a bar and sit my tight, tiny ass on a barstool.

Of course, given the shape I was in, I did get a lot of attention. And putting that barstool under my ass was the best feeling. And I got a good, wet feeling from a guy who was there. My girlfriend warned me about him, but I did him anyway. I was just turned on. This did not turn out well; he was married.

THE MAN IN BLACK

Some friends were going to a dance bar called Bushwhackers; who thinks of these names? I knew how to dance most line dances and couple's dances.

At one point, I noticed a guy across the room. He was dressed all in black—shirt, jeans, and cowboy hat. He looked sexy. *Heaven forbid*, I thought, *I need him*. My sex drive was getting all worked up.

He noticed me back. He nodded and came over. I was completely gaga over him. I wanted this man, and I was very excited that he liked me and wanted me. We went out to my car and made out only. We made a date and, of course, had sex, and that was all she wrote. I was sold. I had to have him—morning, noon, and night.

Sometimes I would be so excited I'd just bend over and say, "Fuck me, hard and fast." No, I'm not talking about anal, just him fucking me from behind.

Well, of course, he had no money, so I paid all the time. I just needed the sex from him. After about three months, I was getting tired of paying and ready for our time together to end. Somewhere in between the sex and the fucking, I had learned that, when he talked, he wasn't very smart and, when he took his hat off, he wasn't so good-looking. He had no money. But he fucked so well that I found myself saying, "Keep your hat on. Don't talk. Just fuck."

Soon that got boring too. I had to end things.

My cowboy in black did do one thing for me. He knew about a program designed to teach you to protect your assets. He thought that, by attending it, he was going to get rich. He asked me to pay his way for a year, promising that, in a year or so, he would be able to take care of me through this program. What a joke!

He introduced me to a group leader, a chiropractor from Bend.

He assigned me to a guy named Bill, so I was under Bill—no, not literally. I went to a meeting and found it very interesting. Of course, since I had work and money, I joined the movement. The guy with the hat who I'd told not to talk but to keep his hat on and just fuck—saying that feels good—did not have any money, so he could not join. How he intended to make money was anyone's guess. But I knew I could make money.

THE PROGRAM

The program had a meeting scheduled in Portland. The founder of the program, Dr. Vanlin, would be in town to talk at this one. I had to be there.

I met Bill in Portland. We watched Dr. Vanlin on the stage. He was so exciting to watch and listen to. He was brimming with charisma and had a great head of thick, gray hair. He was a big guy, but you could tell by looking at him that he had lots of class. My mind wandered as I was thinking of the things I could do to him and with him. Did I really hear him talk? Maybe I was just was imagining him and me.

I was on a mission to meet him and be with him. But who was I? I was an average person. I had looks, but I wasn't educated. Let me clear this up. I was so commonsense smart that I could talk to anyone; well maybe my looks helped too.

FIJI

The next seminar was going to be in Fiji. And little did I know how much this was going to change my life. I paid my $1,500 and bought my ticket to Fiji for the week of the seminar. I found that the program aligned with everything I felt about life and helping people. It offered a way to protect people's assets and keep them from losing their homes through trusts. It was just a great program.

Of course, the government did not like this. Heaven forbid, people should try and protect their assets. Even though the program was completely legal, showing people how to use the law library to save on taxes, the government fought it. This is because the government isn't about the people; it's about how much the government can take from the people. That's my opinion.

I met some great people in Fiji. I talked with speakers from all over the world. Twenty-two speakers attended the seminars. I found Dr. Vanlin very interesting, and I watched him, trying to get his attention. Who was I anyway?

I met a couple of ladies, Lynne and Gayle, and would sit with them. Lynne was a speaker on trusts. The two were a couple, though you wouldn't know it. They would joke and look at Dr. Vanlin. At one point, they said, "There he is. Go talk to him. He is by himself."

Dr. Vanlin had a girl with him at the seminar, though he did not look happy. The girl was young and pretty and had long hair. She looked boring.

The friends I met at the seminar were very prominent and had money, but they were down to earth. We became very good friends. I respected them and liked them as real people.

I never did go up to talk to Dr. Vanlin.

We flew in on Saturday, and the seminar started on Monday. So during my first few days in Fiji, I had time to go to the beach and enjoy the sun and get a tan. Remember, I had been working on my property and had no body fat, so I looked good in my bikini. Lucky me.

Well, I was lying on my chaise lounge on the beach and I heard a voice. When I looked up, I thought I had died and gone to heaven. Three guys were coming up to me. We talked and laughed and joked around. They sat down, and I learned that they were from Australia and New Zealand and were going to the same seminar I was there for. We decided to go together. I was in heaven. They let me know that a fourth guy would be joining us.

I found out that three of the four were interested in me. We would go to the seminar and sit together. I had two guys on either side of me. One side of the room was for people from other countries, and the other side was for attendants from the States. I still sat with the guys. What girl wouldn't?

One of the guys would walk me to my room at night, and we would make out very passionately. We would sometimes sit and watch the sunset. He was a body builder. No, I never had him come into my room. I was very much noticed by everyone, and I had interest in the owner of the co, Dr. Vanlin. I did not want to have rumors flying around about me.

Yes, I had a method to my madness. I didn't have sex with this guy because I had bigger fish to catch. At least this was my plan. I was not going to let anything at the seminars get in the way of that plan, no matter how sex-driven I was.

At one point, I noticed that someone was watching me and following me. It was the guy who had signed me up for the program. I guess he thought I was his for the taking and should be with him the whole week. Gross. He wasn't ugly, but he was kind of nerdy, and I was on a mission.

My, oh my, look how I started. I spent the first few days of the seminar with four gorgeous, well-educated, intelligent men. We exchanged phone numbers and addresses.

The last day, about ten of us spent the whole day together and decided to stay up all night and leave together for the airport at three in the morning. What fun we had.

When I got home, I requested that I be removed from Bill's group and assigned to someone else. I went from one bad apple to the next. I asked to be assigned to Eric, who lived in Vancouver, Washington. I did not know he was Dr. Vanlin's right-hand man.

Eric said he would take me on and that he would set Bill straight with Dr. Vanlin. At first, I thought this new arrangement was great. Everyone liked Eric, and he was in the center of the program.

I couldn't wait to get home and see my two doggies. I had missed them so much. I did call home and leave a message for my doggies.

Of course, I thought they would enjoy hearing my voice. I missed them so much while I was away.

The four guys kept in touch with me. The body builder called me, and our conversation and the energy between us was intense. He wanted to have phone sex. I had never done this before and had never wanted to. But the energy was so high. He started talking and asking me to lie down with nothing on. He had me touch myself on my face and then run my hand over my body. His voice got me incredibly excited. He had me put my hand on my clit, yes the button we sometimes call "oh my God."

Yes, he was good, and I believe we were both sweating and hot and orgasmic. That was one phone call I would never forget.

He was seeing someone, and it would be difficult for him to come to the States. I would go to Fiji a few more times and see him. Later in the chapter, you will know why I did not get together with him.

GARY, THE DENTIST: THIS MAN WAS REAL

I was dating Gary, a dentist, at the time. He probably was the only real guy I ever dated. I loved him for that, and he knew this. We had great sex of course. He had a big fishing boat moored down at the waterfront. I loved being on that boat and lying naked on the deck. I would clean his boat, and his pipes. I loved it.

Gary and I had a great time together. The time we spent together on that boat was the most real, down-to-earth, honest fun I ever had dating someone.

Gary was not a hands-on fix-it man. I was gutting my home at the time. I took a saw- saw to the ceiling. I painted the interior with a paint sprayer and roller. Gary thought he would help. I was very surprised. This was something he had never done before and probably would never do again. He was up on a ladder painting and really going at it.

I was sleeping on a sleeping bag on the floor between the bathroom and the hall. He said he wanted to stay, and he did.

I had to end things with Gary, though. Why? Well, I hired several guys to help with the work on my house. I'd always thought that, if a guy drives up in a car with three wheels, you shouldn't hire him. But I hired these guys anyway.

I could have done a better job than these three guys did, and I would point out mistakes and have them redo things. They may have put in a good bid, but remember the car. That should have told me, I believe, how good they were, or weren't.

One day, Gary and I went to lunch. He pointed his finger at me and told me I needed to fire those guys. He said, while shaking his finger, that if I didn't, he would. It was my house, my money, and my work. Did I need a boss? No. So I ended it.

I told him that I realized that most of the girls he had dated were very young and inexperienced. I could see him shaking his finger with them, but that would not work with me. I did not need a boss or someone telling me what to do. He understood and had been told this before.

We stayed friends and still are. Gary was one of the special guys I dated, one of few.

CHAPTER ELEVEN

RUDY, (DR. VANLIN): HOW I HAD THE LIFE PEOPLE DREAM ABOUT AND HOW WE MET

THE PROGRAM HAD A TRAINING class in Lake Tahoe. I bought my ticket and signed up for the training. I had a great time in Tahoe. I found a local bar with a good-looking bartender. I had his attention every time I went in. I became friends with an older gentleman named Cessal. He was a country man, and his wife had just passed away. We hung out together. I had a few other suitors too.

One was a man who worked in Dr. Vanlin's office. Yes, I did get my share of attention, as much as ten women.

During our classes, Dr. Vanlin seemed to tease me. He'd put me on the spot and ask me to answer questions. I watched him, and he seemed to be there by himself. I wanted to go up and talk to him, but I never did. *Who am I?* I thought. I was just a simple person.

I did have so much fun at the training. I seemed to get all the attention, and I just enjoyed myself.

Next, we had a meeting in Seattle for the marketers to help us promote the program. I drove up by myself and had planned on driving back the same night. A few people who I was signing up for the program attended the meeting.

Dr. Vanlin was there to talk. I always thought his talks were very interesting. Eric was there and ready for me to start selling, so that he could get his share of what I would bring in.

After the meeting, everyone planned to go to a bar and socialize. I was invited. Even though I needed to get on the road, I decided to join them for a bit. David Voth, who I'd met in Fiji, was one of the speakers from Canada. Nicely put, David was very loud and jolly. While I was sitting with them, Dr. Vanlin came in. They introduced me, and he asked me to call him Rudy. We all talked and joked around. David encouraged me to stay instead of driving home. He said I could share his room or someone else's. He commented jokingly that Rudy had a big suite.

Rudy said I could stay on the couch and then have breakfast with all them in the morning. He assured me that I would be safe and need not worry. He wouldn't try anything. He told me to just come and look at his room and then decide.

I walked with him to his room; it was big and had a separate bedroom where I could stay. He wanted me to feel comfortable, and he was very kind and thoughtful. I agreed to stay.

He made out the couch, and I lay down. Soon, I heard a voice. Rudy was checking to see if I was okay. He also let me know that I had a choice; I could sleep on the bed if I wanted to—only to sleep.

I went into the bedroom and lay down. Rudy had a cold and apologized. We started to snuggle, and then we kissed some. The kissing was so good that I decided to do what was the natural thing for me to do. I went right for his cock. I say cock because, when I reached down and put my hand on his crotch, I went, "Oh my

God." I was scared to death. Even with the number of dicks I had felt, I wasn't sure what I was feeling. Rudy's cock was as huge as a donkey's.

I could not sleep. He went on to sleep, and I lay there, afraid of what was under the sheets.

The next morning, we all had a great breakfast and visited. Rudy got my phone number and said he would call and we could get together soon. He did call, and we talked a few times.

One night, he called and said he was coming to see me. He had a girl there, and things between them were not working out. She was sleeping in the other room. She basically was there to get money. He sent her on her way the next day and called me and said he had plane reservations. He would see me in two weeks. I was both excited and nervous.

I picked him up at the airport, and we went back to my place. Later, we met with Eric and his wife for dinner. Rudy and I had so much fun laughing and joking around. I had a life like I never had before—filled with money and class. It was the life so many people dream about. Our sex was fun; even though his cock was giant, it went in me. I thought that, if I was with anyone else after that, his cock would just fall into my cunt.

We did find that he would lose a hard-on if he was lying down. If we stood up, he stayed hard. I discovered that I could use both my hands to jerk him off. My arms were in good shape. He was good orally. Kisses were so good too. We had fun.

I had a ticket for an Alaskan Cruise. Rudy said he would give me the money for it, but I said no. Even though I had my own room, I stayed with Rudy.

During these months, I had my cabin in the woods. Once, Rudy said he was sending me something. He told me to be sure to be home and kept calling to make sure I would be there to receive this very big package. As the time came for the package to arrive, I was anxiously waiting. I tried to guess what it could be. Maybe a new car?

The knock came at my door. I opened it, and there was Rudy standing there naked with a big smile on his face. I was happy to see him, though maybe a little disappointed to find no car. But what a nice surprise.

I was selling my home, and Rudy thought we should live together. He had Eric find us a million-dollar house in West Linn.

I went from being average to having class. It was an entirely different world that I was about to live in—one that consisted of traveling all over the world and having the best of everything. Eric, Rudy's right-hand man, found us a million-dollar home in West Lynn, and we moved in. Rudy would take me into Nordstrom and buy me an entire wardrobe. He told me to get rid of my old clothes—that he would replace them, and he did. Every time we walked through Nordstrom, he just wanted to spend money on me. One time, he had me sit at the Clarins makeup counter, and he bought the entire line—a thousand dollars' worth of makeup.

I did say he should stop spending so much on me until we were further along in the relationship. He thought I was nuts; he wanted to spend the money and did.

We decorated our beautiful home elegantly. He had his furniture brought up from Balboa Island, where his condo was.

For our first Christmas together, we put up a big tree and had a big Christmas party. Rudy said he had to take me somewhere. We got in the car. When he pulled into a car dealership, he said simply, "Pick one out." Oh my God, what was happening? I picked out a new white Jeep Grand Cherokee Limited, fully loaded. He wrote a check and put the Jeep in my name. I have never gotten over that one. I also had quite the gift under the tree—a gold watch that he'd paid a thousand dollars for. He just did not stop.

Everyone thought he was my soul mate. At first I did too. He did all the cooking, and I cleaned. He was so much fun. We just enjoyed life together. He had a great life. Together, we took five cruises, flew to Fiji four times, and vacationed in the Bahamas. My bags were always packed.

What could go wrong?

Well, we got settled in our big home on the hill overlooking the Willamette River. Rudy started saying, "Let's fix up one of the bedrooms."

"Okay," I agreed, "let's."

But he wanted a two-way mirror put on the wall over the dresser. The other side of the wall was the furnace room. "What for?" I asked.

He thought it would be great if I would bring home a friend now and then to fuck—while he watched from the other room. I was shocked. He had mentioned this before we'd moved in together, but I'd thought he was joking. No, he wasn't.

We bought ten thousand dollars' worth of furniture, including a sleigh bed. The room was great. Now the pressure was on. I could not believe what he was asking me. I told him, "I am monogamous. I do not want to have sex with other men."

The pressure was too much, and I turned cold. All he could say was that he wanted his Marilyn back.

Once when we were out in downtown Portland at the waterfront and sitting at the bar, a friend of mine, Mike, came up and said hi to me. I introduced him to Rudy. As Mike and I were talking, Rudy looked at Mike and told him that, if he wanted to take me home, it was okay with him. Mike looked at me in shock.

Yes, he meant it. I was so upset and hurt.

I started to see a psychologist. I told her that I did not want to talk about Rudy. I just wanted to address why I always attracted the same kind of men. During my third visit, she said we had to talk about Rudy.

I said, "I know."

I went home and told him that this was not what I wanted and that I would leave if he continued. He stopped.

Rudy and I got tickets to see a play in Portland called *Tony n'* *Tina's Wedding*. We got a group together, and six more friends would be sitting with us.

Rudy thought I should have a special dress, so we went to a vintage store downtown, and he bought this great 1930s dress for $150. It was black lace from the top to below the waist with a sheer skirt underneath. He wanted me to wear it to the play with nothing on underneath, and I did! The play was interesting, and we had a great time. I always had to keep in mind that I had nothing on beneath my dress. I did find some nude undergarments so that I would look nude.

Rudy and I were headed to Florida, where he was putting on a seminar. One of the last seminars that Rudy was able to attend was the Caribbean Cruise leaving Ft. Lauderdale on Sunday April 11, 1999. We were then headed to Lugano, Switzerland, where he had a second home. I was so excited. We would leave straight after the seminar, once the cruise ship had docked back in Ft. Lauderdale.

FT. LAUDERDALE: OUR FIFTH CRUISE (SO EXCITING)

About four or five hundred people attended the seminar, which featured twelve speakers. Stopping at all the ports was a riot. Rudy, of course, always had the best suite, with a living room, a separate bedroom, and a huge bathroom. We would entertain at the suite, hosting meetings and happy hour with the speakers. Rudy was waiting for money to come in from Switzerland to pay the speakers. I loved that everyone was so happy.

On April 15, we tried to call my son to wish him a happy birthday, and could not get a connection out on the phones on the dock. Little did we know what he could have told us.

We docked. In order to get everyone off the cruise ship on time, we had to be packed and have our luggage outside the door by 9:00 a.m. for pick up. We had not packed anything the night before; Rudy said we would just do it in the morning. Around 7:00 a.m., we heard a knock on the door. Still undressed, we answered. Two men came in and grabbed Rudy and put handcuffs on him. They sat him at the dining table. I was panicking. FBI agents were placing Rudy under arrest. I did not know what to do. We were supposed to be off the ship now.

I went out of the room in search of help. Panicking, I searched the ship for someone that could come to our aid. I could not find anyone; everyone was out of the rooms and waiting for checkout. I looked for my good friend, Lynne, who had been a speaker at the seminar, but I couldn't find her. Feeling helpless, I called Lynne. She said she would meet me when we got off the ship.

I found Rudy's travel agent, and she came to my room to help me. As we threw all of our things into the suitcases, I wondered what was happening to Rudy. The FBI agents had taken him down below to a room.

We got off the ship. The agents told me they were taking Rudy to a holding cell in downtown Ft. Lauderdale. I had no money. Rudy had booked the cruise. Lynne said she would get a room for us to stay in. Her other half left and went back home to Newport Beach, California. We ran all over town looking for an attorney. Meanwhile, the court set a hearing date. Eric stayed a few days also.

The entire experience was so awful that my voice was shutting down. I could barely talk. With all this negativity, I wound up with no voice at all. Lynne talked for me and paid for my needs while we were in Florida, as well as my ticket home. We found an attorney who would stand in for Rudy and went to the hearing. Well, ours being a corrupt system and one that is not for the people, of course things didn't go well.

We heard the FBI agent say, "Judge, we have nothing on him. We have been following him for a year and a half and have not come up with anything. But, Judge, if you hold him, we will find something."

Now how could that be right? A year and a half and they had nothing. The agents planned to take him back to LA and hold him in jail there. As I would learn, they escorted him all the way from Florida to Los Angeles by bus, a strategy they use when they are trying to break people.

Rudy called when he arrived in LA; he got one call. He told me he'd had basically no food or water, that he'd been chained, and that the trip had zigzagged back and forth across the United States so that he wouldn't know where they were—as if he was on the most wanted list as a murderer. He told me a hearing had been set for the next day. He knew what to say because he had talked about this scenario at the seminars.

When I talked to him next, he said the FBI agent had promised him that everything would be okay if he would just sign a document admitting to things that he did not do. The FBI agent said it would not be used against him because they still hadn't found anything on him. It was outright persecution. When Rudy told me that he had signed the document, I was furious. He said that he wished he hadn't, but the agent had approached him on his first night off the bus and he'd been disoriented from the trip. I had read and heard that our government used methods like this to control people and get what they wanted, right or wrong.

Months and months of court hearings ensued. I stayed in California with Lynne so that I could go to the hearings. I also just wanted to be close so I could take advantage of any possibilities of seeing Rudy. It was a nightmare. We were all so helpless in the fight to help him.

I was still living in the big million-dollar home in West Linn. Rudy's daughter would send me five thousand dollars a month to live on. I had Rudy's car and mine.

One evening, I heard a noise outside my bedroom. When I looked out, I saw Eric outside the bedroom patio doors. He had some big, long-handled tools. I went to the door. Was I an idiot or what?

I let him in. He wanted the keys to Rudy's car. When I told him no, he threatened to jump-start the car. Eric said that his daughter had called and told him to go get the car and hide it. I think she might have been on wacky tobacco.

Why did I not call the police? Why did I let him in? I was so frustrated, and I knew that Rudy would be calling me that evening to set things straight.

He did. Eric, however, would not bring the car back. I had to have someone take me downtown to pick the car up.

I knew I had to move. I did not know how long Rudy's daughter would keep sending me money to pay the bills. I arranged to meet with Rudy and his attorney and had Rudy sign his car over to me, as well as the rental agreement, so that we could get out of the lease, which was more than three thousand dollars a month.

I told the company that Rudy was ill in a hospital in LA and could not call or come back to our home, adding that I was going to move there. The company let me out of the lease, and I got the car title transferred to my name. I put half of everything in storage and sold the rest, including most of Rudy's furniture. Consumer Northwest, a consignment store, picked up the furniture. Rudy had a lot of expensive stuff, including a dining table he'd paid $16,000 for. The consignment store sold it for $6,000; that's how much I got anyway.

Wow, I made a lot of backup money to live on. Rudy had already given his kids a car, so he said his was mine. And he understood about everything else. We had bought some Persian rugs at $5,000 or more apiece. I took them back to Meir and Frank for a refund, saying that the size of the rugs was wrong for our home. I collected a lot of money. I did not tell Rudy immediately when I moved out of the house, so the $5,000 checks coming in for the next three or four months. I saved the money for a down payment on a condo.

I'm sorry to say that I took all of his clothes to Eric and left the bundle in a hallway in front of the office we had in downtown Portland. I kept Rudy's watch and coins of value and sold them.

Of course, I did all this only after Rudy was sentenced to serve five years in prison. And he was serving time for nothing, by the way. The government and FBI agents had made up stories to keep him in prison for the simple reason that he was running a great program that taught people how to protect their assets and minimize their taxes the right way. It was all legal. Tax avoidance is legal; tax evasion is illegal.

Heaven forbid, someone who knew the law should be on the streets helping people. Everything Rudy encouraged people to do followed the guidance of the laws that were on the books. Go to a law library and check it out. But the government has bigger guns and couldn't afford to have great men like Rudy out there.

CHAPTER TWELVE

FROM A CONDO IN LAKE OSWEGO TO A HOME IN NEWPORT

I STARTED MAKING ARRANGEMENTS TO BUY a condo in Lake Oswego with a down payment of $45,000. I had been saving money and needed a home. I put $15,000 down and would owe the remainder of the payment when I moved in.

Meanwhile, my daughter was in the process of a divorce, and she would be losing her house due to past due mortgage payments. She needed to make the payments in order to get a loan. I told her I would send her $18,000 of my down payment as long as she could get it back to me before closing. She said she was sure she could do that. She gave me a phone number so I could call and confirm her loan. The institution assured me that everything was ready to go. Once I paid her back mortgage payments, she would have the loan.

What a nightmare. I didn't get the money back, and my daughter quit answering her phone. I was panicking. Where was I going to come up with the balance I needed to move into the condo?

I went to the Oswego Point Condos representative who was selling me the condo and told him I needed to stop the loan from going through. According to our contract, I had thirty days to change my mind, and it was day twenty-eight. He said we could go ahead and cancel the contract if that was what I wanted to do but made me an offer. He would hold the condo for a while longer, and if I still couldn't come up with the balance, I wouldn't lose any money.

I tried to gather the funds I needed but couldn't. What a nasty situation that turned out to be. The guy was completely dishonest. He now said that, if I did not come up with the balance of $25,000, I would lose what I had put down. I was sick. I had new furniture being held everywhere waiting to be moved in when I got the condo.

I put my mind to work and borrowed $15,000 off my jeep. That's when I learned from my friend who was my mortgage broker that my payments for the condo, which I'd thought were going to be $950 a month, had gone to $1,400 a month. The payments for the loan off the jeep would be $450 a month. I could no longer afford the condo. My daughter still didn't know how she could get me the $18,000, along with $5,000 I'd loaned her to get her car back after it had been repossessed.

The situation snowballed into a $150,000 loss. I had spent all of my retirement funds. I sold my garage for $10,000 and put that toward the condo. I sold my beautiful furniture for another $10,000, which I also put toward the condo. In the end, my payments for the condo went from $950 to $1,800 a month. On top of that I had to pay the $450 a month for the jeep loan. My expenses were close to $1500 a month higher than what I'd planned for. I had lost my condo and all my money.

DENNIS: TALL, GORGEOUS, AND NICE TOO

While I was getting all moved out and staying with my son, I went out with some friends at the Harbor Side in downtown Portland. We were sitting at the bar on my favorite seat—a barstool. My friends and I were talking and eating. This gorgeous man came up to talk to my girlfriend, who was sitting next to me.

I just let them talk and finished eating my appetizer. I heard a voice, and again I turned and looked up. This gorgeous man was talking to me. He said he would love to talk to me and get together sometime. I said, "Me?" I was shocked, but he said yes and asked if I would like that.

After I got myself together, I said yes. He was tall with coal black hair and blue eyes, my favorite combination, and he had a great body. I always dreamed of men like him, but they never asked me out.

As it turned out, Dennis was an ex-boyfriend of a girl I knew. He said that would not be a problem. We got together at his friend's in Portland because he lived in Bend. I would go there and visit, and we had great sex, wonderful sex, as well as great kissing.

Dennis was incredibly nice and had his act together. I did not tell him I was still with Rudy in a sense. I was still putting on seminars and talking to Rudy on the phone. I had to take the calls. I couldn't tell Rudy about Dennis either. Though he might be okay with me seeing Dennis, he would ask me about the sex and want details.

The first time I went to Bend, my feelings for Dennis were strong. He was making great plans for my arrival—a special dinner with candlelight. I believed he was going to ask me to marry him. I did not go that Friday; I found an excuse not to. I did go the next day, and we had a great time. Being with him felt the way one should feel with someone. But I felt he was coming on too strong. What was wrong with me?

I knew he was nice. I'd talked to his ex-girlfriend. They'd been together for six years, and she only had good things to say about him. And I felt great with him, kind of like being in a dream world and yet down to earth at the same time.

One thing I knew for sure was that the money I had coming in was not going to last. Dennis thought it was okay for me to travel; he did not like to travel, but he would trust me to do my work. Of course, the lifestyle I'd grown accustomed to would not last long, and I knew he looked at that as part of what I had to offer; I could pay my half. I was flattered and surprised. I started backing off.

Caretaker: Newport, Oregon, at the Beach

I decided that I'd had enough of being single in Portland. Every time I went out, I would see the same men. I took out an ad in the paper offering my services as a caretaker.

I got a call from a retired doctor and his wife, who lived in Newport, Oregon. I went to meet them; they had built a home for a caregiver two years earlier so that they would never have to go to a nursing home. The house was on a hill overlooking Embarcadero Hotel and the bay and the ocean. What a view, and the house was beautiful. The job would include rent and utilities plus pay in exchange for three days a week for four hours and dinner two nights a week.

Ernie asked when I would like to start, and I said yesterday. The day I was there for the interview was my birthday, February 16, 2001.

I was selling my condo, so I was ready to move. I packed up and headed for Newport. I was so excited to be living at the beach. The job included taking care of the yard, cleaning the house, and learning to cook the meals Ernie and Mildred liked.

Ernie was a man who no one liked; he wanted things his way and that was it. Mildred was a yes-wife; whatever Ernie wanted was okay and whatever he told her to do, she did. I am not a yes-woman and will not be talked down to. Ernie and I would work in the yard some days. He liked the shrubs trimmed just right. I help Mildred in the house one day a week.

One day, Ernie put his cane in a shrub and said, "Cut that piece off that branch—just a nip."

I told him that, if he kept doing that with his cane, I was going to nip it off. I just held my ground, and I earned his respect. He thought

I was his buddy, I guess. One Saturday, he was going fishing at 5:00 a.m. and asked if I would like to go. That was sweet. He wanted me as a fishing buddy, as he had no friends.

I would meet the town people and neighbors up on the hill, and they would tell me stories about how rude Ernie was and how badly he had treated people when he was a doctor in the hospital. He treated his neighbors badly too. They thought I must be a saint to still be working for him. All the other people he'd hired had only lasted a month, maybe two, and had just left.

When I first moved in, I got the cable hooked up. A man came to the door to do the install, and all of a sudden three or four men were there. One guy asked if I would like to meet him for a drink. He was cute, so I thought, why not?

There seemed to be a lot of utilities workers around my house the first month I moved in. I found out that I was the new girl in town. It was a beach town, so not many new women were around to meet. All the single men were checking me out. This was fun for me.

The first time I decided to go to town to see what Newport had to offer in terms of the single life, I had driven just five minutes when I came to the main street. I started down it, and soon I saw a lot of cars and came to a bar, the Rouge, that seemed to be crowded with people.

I parked and went in; the place was packed. Did I hit it lucky. My first Friday night out, and I'd hit the jackpot. I sat at the bar and met the bartender, Bruce, who was nice-looking and married. We became friends. In no time, I was talking to other people at the bar and had become friends with all the locals. I met Amy and her husband Jim. They ran the brewery.

Everyone took me in. It wasn't long before I became a regular. Customers would come in, and I would always be sitting at the bar, so they'd think I was a local too. This was nice. I got invited to all the functions in town. Amy said she had never seen anyone come to town and be invited to all the main town functions before.

A big dinner was being held at one of the main hotels for all the employees of the Rouge brewery. It was black-tie. Amy called and asked if I would fill in and be a date for an employee. Of course I said yes. I had so much fun, and my blind date, Chris, was nice. He wasn't bad looking either, but he was poor and nice. We became friends too.

Amy was trying to set us up, and we had a few dates. But he was too nice and too poor for me. Yes, we did go to bed. He kissed well, but when we got to bed and started kissing, he came. Yes, it was over that quickly. It had been a long while for him, and he was so excited to be in bed with me—the new girl in town. Well, that was it for me. We still got together as friends.

I must say, Chris did something that was so sweet and cute. I had a dog, named Maxwell, and Chris got him a Christmas present. He made a treat can out of a Maxwell coffee can and filled it with treats. The gesture was so sweet.

I went into the Rogue about three times a week. Maybe the bar was home week for all the regulars who lived in Newport. I met a lot of guys in there and went to bed with many. I was being asked out by married men. I thought after the tenth one that I was going to scream. I became friends with a nice man, Mark, who was married to Gabrielle, the granddaughter of the Moe's clam chowder owner. I desired Mark so much that I would just sit in my window and look across the bay where he and Gabrielle lived. I thought he should be mine. We always flirted, and our flirtations were so hot. I was obsessed with him, and he with me. We talked about having sex together. I was wet all the time from wanting him. I planned to have sex with him, but in the end, I couldn't go there.

CHAPTER THIRTEEN

BACK TO PORTLAND

E VENTUALLY, IT WAS TIME TO move on from Newport. In 2002, I rented a U-Haul truck with a trailer to pull my car and headed back toward Portland. I found an apartment in Beaverton, located at 4130 SW 117th. It was a nice place to move into, and I was happy to be back home.

REVEREND MARY'S STALKER

I started going to church again at the Living Enrichment Center. It was a great church. I loved going there. It provided me another way to just feel into life. I had first attended the Enrichment Center in 1990, and I felt from the heart when I was there.

I had never met anyone to date at the church. One day, though, I noticed a guy who was sitting next to Reverend Mary Manning Morrissey. I started to watch him. I thought that, if he was sitting next to her, he must be okay. Maybe I should never think.

He and I started to go out. He had no money, but he seemed nice. The sex was great; he knew his moves with his mouth, and his fucking was great. Damn, he was good. But something was wrong with him; I could feel it.

One morning, I was sitting on my couch, and I heard a noise on my sliding glass door. It was him standing out there with a coffee drink. I did not know what to think, so I just said, "Thanks."

We did a few things together. He did not work and was different. A friend of mine at the church warned me to watch out. It seemed he had formerly been stalking Mary, the minister, thinking she wanted to be with him. Then I guess we had gotten together and he'd turned his attentions to me.

He told me a story about how hurt he'd been when his last girlfriend had ended their relationship. To get back at her, he'd decided to fake his death. He went to her garage and hung himself; he knew from being in the service how to tie knots. She came into the garage and screamed and ran back into the house and called 9-1-1. When the emergency responders arrived and they went back into the garage, he was gone.

After hearing that story, I knew I should not talk with him again. He had answered what I'd been trying to figure out. I knew now that he wasn't just weird; he was sick. I ignored him at all cost at the church, pretending as best I could that he did not exist.

In 2003, I moved to Gresham. Then in 2004, I moved back to Beaverton, in a place off of Allen and Murray.

JOHN NUMBER TWO: A PRETENSE TO CONVERT ME TO MORMONISM

It was back in 1996 that I first learned about the program and began traveling and attending seminars, learning and teaching people how to protect their assets the legal way. At one point, my son worked for a guy named John. When my son mentioned that his mom was in a movement working toward non-taxation or minimizing taxes, John was very interested. He wanted to go to a meeting.

We had a big meeting set up at our downtown Portland office. Some fifty to a hundred people would be in attendance, along with a variety of different speakers. My son invited John. I had not met him yet.

When I met him, I was impressed. John was a family man, with a good heart and a great body. I thought that having someone like him would be great.

At the meeting, I learned that John was very much into the government issues we were discussing. He knew a lot about what we were doing and our strategies for helping people not lose their homes. Talking to him was great.

John joined our group and planned on going to our upcoming seminars. The next one scheduled was an Alaskan cruise. I made good money on that one again. Each time you signed people up to be part of the movement, you got a percentage of his or her enrollment fees. Sweet John brought his dad on the cruise, so he did not visit with us much. Rudy had not been with us on that cruise. As you know, he was in prison.

Time went by, and I started getting e-mails from John saying that he would love to take me to Greece or the Caribbean Islands. I did not know what was going on, as John was married. This man did not seem the type to send me this kind of e-mail. He didn't come across as a cheater. He came across as a man who would be true to one woman.

I e-mailed him back, just to make contact with him and to avoid being rude. Plus, I really wanted to know what was going on.

To my surprise, he was divorced and had thought of me for five years. He said he'd loved me since the first time he met me but had been unable to do anything about it because he'd been married.

Yes, I did want a date with him. I thought that he might be the perfect man—the man of my dreams. He was nice-looking, kept his body in good shape, and was a family man. What else would I want?

I made a date with him. I was so excited to finally be going out with a man who I thought might be the one—someone I would be proud to be with. This was, unlike all the others, not just about sex. I thought maybe John could be a real partner. I did dream and hope, and I was always trying to improve myself and attract the right man, someday.

With all my anticipation about my first real date with John, I barely remembered what he looked like.

The doorbell rang. When I opened the door, I found, to my surprise, that I was not sure about his look. He had redder hair than I remembered, and he was shorter. His skin was fair—not something that would usually get my attention. He came in, and we talked a little before leaving for our dinner date.

When we got to the parking lot, he opened the car door for me. His car was nice and new, which was good, as I like nice things. I was impressed. As we were driving, he told me that he had just gotten the car to drive for the day so that he could decide if he would like to buy it. I knew that he'd gotten the car to impress me. Later, I would see his old car, which he could not part with. It ran, but I was not impressed. That was why he had the loaner car for the night.

We had a great dinner date and good conversation. Later in the evening, we were on our way back to my place. I suggested that we stop for a drink and talk. He thought it was a good idea. We went into a bar, and I ordered a drink but he did not. Then he said that he didn't drink, but that was okay. A ways into the conversation, he explained that he was Mormon—okay, that didn't bother me—and that he had never had a drink. Nor had he ever bought a drink for anyone; I was the first. Hmm, that was different; for me, most dating was based on sharing a drinking out or staying in with a glass of wine.

But his abstinence from alcohol didn't bother me too much. I'm not much of a drinker anyway; I'm a lightweight.

We got back to my place and started talking on the couch. Before long, we were making out. I asked him to stay, and he said yes. Here we go again—another man and sex on the first date. This would tell me whether or not we should date. Wasn't that how it worked?

We got into bed, and he felt so good. He was so gentle and sensual when it came to lovemaking. A lot of men forget this part and go straight to their cock. John definitely wanted to see me and planned on marrying me. He said I was the one he wanted. I was impressed—a man who knew what he wanted.

John and I started dating regularly, and soon we were together all the time. He made plans for us to go visit the Street of Dreams. We went, and looking at all the homes and hearing him talk about wanting ideas for the home he wanted to build for us was so romantic. We picked out the most expensive one there with a pool.

We danced as we went into some of the houses. He would twirl me around, and we laughed and talked. I knew I wanted to be with him and never lose this feeling.

John liked to eat. He took me to many events and festive functions in Oregon that revolved around food. We'd eat different foods and visit with all kinds of people. We had so much fun.

We went to Multnomah Falls to have dinner. The evening was so romantic that I just got carried away in the moment and said, "John, I want to marry you."

He said, "Yes, that will happen."

You see, I had never wanted to marry again—never.

I had always gotten married for sex; if the sex was good, I'd figure me and whoever I was sleeping with must be good—until I got to know him. Then I would start shutting down. I would discover that he was not nice or that he was dishonest; or maybe he liked to argue or to cheat. After a while, I would let the man of the hour know what would work for me—what I needed if we were going to make it. You see, I always let the men I was with be themselves and hoped they would figure out what I needed. I flowed with them and catered to them, in the hope that they would see me, not the cunt part of me—spread my legs and they were happy—but the me with a heart, who wanted to care in a real way. I was learning, and I just wanted a real relationship, one that worked for both partners, not just one.

This man seemed different. And yes, I got caught up in the moment right away. The sex was good but not the best. Still, everything else was there, and I could teach him about sex. I was good and knew what a man's body wanted, and I sure knew what my body wanted, liked, and needed.

John was Mormon, and I had heard that oral sex was not allowed. That would not work for me. I liked and needed oral sex. My cunt craved it. I liked having my own cock, one that was the right size and the right fit. I like looking at one and feeling it, sucking and pleasing my own cock, my man, for both of us.

About three months into my whirlwind relationship with John, I started noticing that he wasn't all he said he was. I really started listening to him and asking questions, making sure I understood what he meant when he said something. He loved my family, and I had not met any of his. I asked what was wrong. He would just say it wasn't the right time yet; he would arrange a time for us to meet.

Then he did invite me to meet his secretary of twenty years, who was also his ex-sister-in-law. She said the family had wanted to meet me too. She was great. We agreed that he was a little secretive about his life.

That he had not gotten over his wife, who had left him for a lover she'd had for the last ten years of their marriage, was obvious. She was married again. But she and John had stayed friends, which was good for the kids.

When would I get to meet the kids? I hadn't met John's kids yet, and we were planning a life together. How could we share a life if I hadn't met his family? So many red flags were cropping up; they were starting to amount to a big list.

Finally, I got to meet his daughter and then his son. I liked them, and they liked me.

A family gathering was planned for the christening of his son's baby. The entire family would be going to southern Oregon for this event. I was not invited. John's ex was going, and she would not be taking her husband either.

The son I had not met flew into town for the event, and John did invite me to meet him. The son looked at me and asked if I was planning on going to the family reunion. I looked at him and said that I was not invited. He was shocked. I looked at John and said again, "Your dad did not invite me."

John's son replied, "That's not right. I'm inviting you, so please do come to meet the family. I would really like you to be there.

Finally John spoke up and said that he agreed; it would be good for me to go.

I did not go.

A few months had gone by, and my list of questions about John and who he really was was getting long. I wanted the man he presented himself to be, but as time went by, he did not do any of the things that he said he was. Rather, he seemed just the opposite.

I decided to call and talk to Michelle, his secretary and former sister-in-law. I needed to talk to someone who knew him. I hoped she wouldn't mind.

To my surprise, she did not mind at all. In fact, she asked what had taken me so long to call. She'd thought I would have called weeks earlier.

We had a great talk. When I told her I had a list of thirty issues, she replied, "Is that all?" As I went through my questions, she helped with all of them. Michelle had an answer for all of the issues I raised. His ex-wife had had all the same issues with him, and they had driven her crazy. As a Mormon, he had not wanted a divorce, but he had not been able to see her issues. Finally, she had just left. He had given her everything, including the house and the business, which was worth a million, in the hope that she would change her mind.

I could not go through this either. I sat down to talk to him. I explained that I could not go on like this. It wasn't working for me. "You are not the person you led me to believe you were," I told him. When I asked him why he had done this, he said he wanted me and had hoped I would just fall in love with him.

After I got to know him, I did not think this was going to happen. He was so complicated. He was almost crying as he said that he wanted to work on us.

I said okay. I thought I could work on us too, because I was turning off.

I went for the sex part. It took nine months to teach him to become a great lover and to know a woman's body. He was an eager learner. But even though we had that going, I was still shutting down.

I was now living in Gresham, only a few miles from him, but I had not yet been to his place. My location was good, as I was also only a few miles from my mom. She had been getting worse, and being able to stop by on my way home from work and see her was nice. My work and business were in the southwest area of Portland, and I was driving in the traffic every day each direction. I had never carried coffee in the car while I was driving until then. The traffic was busy and slow, so coffee was good; I needed to have something to do.

I called Michelle and said I wanted to see where John lived and where his business was. Again she asked me what had taken me so long. She told me the best time and day to come over and gave me directions.

I made my way to the address she had provided one morning. I was a little nervous, but this was something I needed to do. When I arrived, John was not there. Michelle said he was normally always there and slept down below the office in the basement. The living space was locked, and we could not get into it.

The office had been converted from an old farmhouse, and it was a pack rat of a place. John's dad lived in another farmhouse on the property, 50 acres worth $3 or 4 million, I was told.

John never showed up, so I left. When John called and we talked, he mentioned that he was sorry he'd missed me and was glad I'd seen the place.

His estate that he took care of for his dad was an old farm in Gresham. His mom had left his dad for one of his dad's best friends when he and his brother were four and five years old. His mom and her new husband moved back east to the mountains. His mom had thought that the boys would be better off and would get the education they needed with the dad. John and his brother had very high IQs and were very knowledgeable in many areas.

I shared this with you so you would know some of John's background. I had compassion for him; he'd had a good life with his dad and grandma and had been raised well. He was well educated. John said as he had no regrets about his mom, but Michelle and I knew he had some insecurities about both his mom and life in general.

I kept turning off and shutting down, which is what I do when I find myself surrounded by negativity. We were together one night and John said, "Honey"—that is what he always called me—"why are you not wanting sex? What is bothering you?"

The next thing he said was the straw that started me looking to really end our relationship. John looked at me and said, "Honey, you will come around. A women needs to take care of her man."

"What do you mean by that?" I demanded.

John explained that a woman is always there for sex; she is ready in the morning or evening. She walks around with no clothes on at home, so she'll be there for her man.

"Is this a Mormon thing?" I asked.

"No, honey," he said. "It is what a woman does for her man."

Wait a minute. We had been having sex all the time. I liked it, but with all the negativity, I had started to shut down. Now after his speech, I didn't want sex at all; he made it sound like an obligation. He was saying that a woman should have sex not because she wanted to be with her man or because she was excited or in the heat of passion. Rather, it was a requirement—something she must do, for her man.

Who in the hell said that? Even though I had taught him well how to be a great lover for me, I did not want to have sex with him at all.

I'd had enough, and I started to plan to move out, as he was paying for my apartment. It was February, and my mom had passed away, so this was definitely a good time to find a place to live back in the west side of Portland, close to my work and friends.

I started a daily search in the paper for an apartment, but I didn't tell John what I was doing. One day, I found an ad for a manager at an apartment complex in the Multnomah Village area. I had always wanted to live in that neighborhood. The company seeking the manager just happened to be one I'd applied for a job with earlier in the year. I faxed my application in, and the company called. I got the job. I still didn't tell John.

I was on the Internet looking for work when an Internet dating ad popped up. I had never before wanted to go there. But something drew me to this site. I just wanted to see what it was all about. I was ending my relationship with my boyfriend and I would be moving soon. So why not just look? I told myself.

I pulled up the Web site and started going down the list, reading about and looking at some of the men who were on the dating site in Portland.

This was something I was meant to see. Talk about being guided to listen to your inner voice. Things happen for a reason.

About the tenth guy I came across was John. There was his

picture. Can you believe this? There was my boyfriend on a dating
site. Was his ego really so big? And was this why he was so secretive?
I read what John had posted about himself. This was not the man I
knew. This was the man he had led me to believe he was, even better.
I wanted to date this man on the dating site. He was too perfect.
Who was he kidding?

He did not know that I was going to end this perfect relationship.
He knew we were going to be together, and I would be his object of
sex twice a day every day as needed; that was what a woman did for
her man, right. He would be surprised to learn that I wasn't going
there.

Needless to say, I was the one who'd gotten a surprise. I could
not imagine John on this site. Why was his profile here?

I did not tell John that I had seen him on the site. I had found
a job that would also give me a home to live in. So I did not have to
come up with money to move.

I sat down to talk to John and told him that I had found a place
to live in southwest Portland. I explained that I needed to move, as
driving back and forth for several hours a day was just too difficult. I
added that he would no longer have to pay my rent but that I needed
him to pay the first month and the deposit fees to get me started. I
still did not tell him—and I didn't plan to tell him until I'd moved—
that I had found him on the site or that I wouldn't have to pay rent.

I needed help in the beginning, and his paying my first month gave
me a cushion to put in the bank. He was fine with the arrangement
I suggested because he had been paying $1,200 a month for my rent
for almost a year. He had never put me on the lease, and I had never
filled out any paperwork when I moved in. I do not know what he
told the landlords about me. Now I did not care.

John rented a U-Haul truck, packed it, and unloaded it. He
wanted to do it all. He was a doer. I was so glad to get into my
apartment and to have this job. It would be such a good move for
me. John got me all moved in. We sat together on the couch, and he

said that he would be over in the next day or two to help. We would still see a lot of each other, and he would be there for me always. I kissed him, and he left. I started to put the apartment together, and being there just felt so good.

As I arranged my new apartment, I felt like I was also rebuilding my new life. You see, it had been a hard few years. My mom had been sick. I'd had one thing after another happening. I felt like I'd experienced the seven-year itch. Then one day in April, I found John's profile on the dating Web site and my job, and it seemed like all my problems with my credit accounts were resolving themselves. I had been getting letters in the mail about issues with my accounts, and it all just stopped. I once again had credit on my accounts. Everything just started to happen smoothly.

I was so happy; this place was exactly where I should be.

This is not the end of John; I still hadn't confronted him about the dating site.

I couldn't wait any longer. Now that I had set myself up in my new apartment, my mind was working overtime. I was trying to decide how to handle things with John. Suddenly, I had it. I wrote a letter, telling him how I had found his online profile before I'd moved and how I'd waited until getting settled in to end our relationship. I printed the ad on the dating site, along with his picture and took the pages to a place where I could use a fax machine. I planned to fax everything to his work. I knew that, even though it was addressed to him, Michelle and the other girls in the office would see it first. I wanted them to know what had happened and to really make a statement about what he'd done.

I got a call from John. He wanted to explain and did not want to end our relationship. He loved me.

His explanation was that he'd put up the profile on the dating site as an experiment. He was curious about how those sites worked; that was all. Being a researcher of all things, he, along with his brother, who was a scientist, was always seeking knowledge.

Now I had heard everything. My life seemed like a never-ending series of stories from different men. I just keep meeting men who were so "different"; if I found a normal one, I would be bored. I wanted to try it out, just to see if I could handle it. I probably couldn't. I wanted a bad boy with a good boy mind and spirit.

I told John that the profile was the last straw and asked him not to call me. He needed to let me go. I needed a break from all the drama.

John stopped calling and asking why. But he e-mailed me frequently for years. He'd call me honey and tell me he still loved me and that he could not let go. He did the same with his ex-wife. He could not let go of her either.

In the end, so that he could understand what I was thinking and what I knew of him, I arranged a time with a psychic I knew in West Linn. I had been going to Susan for years. John went, as he was curious; he had never gone to a psychic before, so this is good. We had an hour with Susan. She talked to me for fifteen minutes and then to John for fifteen minutes; then she spent thirty minutes with the two of us. She taped everything that was said.

John and I got such a better picture of what was going on. I not only felt the answer but got a clear picture of our relationship. When I went first starting seeing the psychic, she said that I had always thought of John as being married. I knew he wasn't, but that is what she felt. Now talking to both of us, Susan told us that he had not let go of his marriage, and that was clear to both of us. She said that John had just started to move on and that, down the road, he would have a place for me. He just didn't now, after a year and a half. According to Susan, John had a lot to finish in order to move forward with someone, but he would get there.

That was what we both needed to move on, at least for John. I am grateful to Susan. Her insight was spot on and what both of us needed.

CHAPTER FOURTEEN

LOSING MY MOM

Before my mom passed away on February 6, 2005, I had talked to her every day. I would call just to hear her voice. If she answered, I knew she was okay, and I could tell from her tone how she was feeling. She had emphysema and bronchitis and had lost half a lung from smoking heavily since she was thirteen years old.

Her husband was sixteen years younger than she was. One time, I asked her why she didn't find someone her age who was retired so they could travel together. She just said, "Yuck; they are old."

She liked sex, and I guess she didn't want someone who could not perform. You see, it started with my mom; being sexual ran in my family. Well, my mom was where I got my addiction from. My mom would tell me that all she wanted was to be loved. I used to wonder what was wrong with her; we loved her. Didn't she get that? Many years later, I discovered that this was me too. We both longed just to be truly loved, for who we were inside and to not need sex to feel loved. I wanted so badly to experience this before I died. I feel that, sadly, I share that desire, that wanting to be loved, with my mom.

THE APARTMENT IN MULTNOMAH VILLAGE, 2005–2007

After my mom died, I had face surgery in April 2005. I had already scheduled the surgery before my mom passed away. I was also planning on moving after she passed. I wanted to move back to the southwest side of town, near my work. I had moved to be close to her and to John. Now that my mom was gone and I had ended my relationship with John, it was time to move.

As I mentioned earlier, in April, I was reading the paper and came across an ad from an apartment company looking for an apartment manager in the southwest Portland area. I had applied with the company a year earlier, but at the time, nothing small enough for what I wanted was available. According to the ad, two complexes were in need of a manager.

I faxed in my résumé, and to my surprise, I got a call from the company. The person I spoke to remembered me from a year earlier. I took a position as apartment manager for the Multnomah Ridge apartment complex, which had twenty-five units and was situated in a good area. This would be perfect for me.

The move into the Multnomah Ridge apartments was very good for me. I found that during the two years plus I was there, I was the most balanced I had ever been. Multnomah Ridge was a good company to work for—no out-of-place hanky-panky, just straight business.

Larry, who was the vice president, did the hiring for apartment managers. He was all about the business and went by the rules; everyone who worked for the company followed suit, so we were all on the same track. This was good. I was trained by the book, and I liked it. I liked both my apartment and my job.

My apartment wasn't fancy, but it was nice. It wasn't classy like some of the places I had lived in before, but it was a good place for me and I met lots of nice people.

Of course there is always someone who defies the rule, but the overall picture was good. One woman who worked in the office was extremely rude to everyone. She thought she ran the show. No one could say anything about her because the owner liked her, so she got away with her rudeness. Everyone in the office just ignored her; we had to deal with her. Every Friday, we would call in our orders for supplies, and again we had to deal with another gal who was very rude to all of us. She talked down to us, and we just had to take it. What a shame; we were all so nice too. We all tried to talk to her as a person, but she just talked down to everyone. She thought this was the way to keep everyone in line and ensure that no one overstepped her. I guess I had to share this to vent about this part of the job, but I still liked my job.

The office people were very nice, and an in-house legal person handled all the company's legal affairs. The job was great. I always went in to turn my work in once or twice a week and visit with Jim. I was proud of my work and who I was. I cleaned and filled the apartment complex up. It was half-empty when I first started. Through my efforts, a lot of nice, middle-class working people moved in.

David: The Dramatic Charmer Who Would Tell You What You Wanted to Hear

I registered a profile on Match.com. If you've ever tried a dating site, you know that the choices are slim. Dating online—or I should say finding a man who is honest, in shape, and of course, not married—is challenging.

I just wanted to meet someone to date. One profile with an e-mail address but no picture caught my attention. I had heard that you should never respond to a profile with no picture. But I did anyway. The message was so intriguing. I e-mailed and asked the guy to send a picture. He did. He was not what I wanted look at to date, but he sounded interesting. He was an investment broker in Lake Oswego.

David and I met for a drink and hit it off. We laughed and had a lot in common, including being the same age. This was nice too. He had the same lifestyle as I wanted with class, money, and a good social life. We met on a Thursday, and we decided to make a date to meet again. He thought Monday would be nice. I was confused. If you are interested and single, the weekend was here, so why not Friday or Saturday?

Well, Monday it was. We met again, and again we had a lot of fun. After meeting a few times, he wanted to come to my home and take some pictures that I wanted for Match. I said okay, and we made plans. I had just watched an Oprah show where she demonstrated how to make her favorite pomegranate martini. I went and bought fancy martini glasses and a shaker at Macy's. I was ready.

David came by to take the pictures and tried my martinis out. He took the pictures, and they looked good. I wore a special dress that I had just bought. Then I made the martinis. We toasted, and they were the best.

We had a few martinis and started joking around. We started kissing and teasing as I do. Well, we just went for it. He took me and fucked me like I had never had it before, or at least in a while.

Wow, now I was hooked. You know my routine. It was the same pattern, like a book. It was sex, just a different name and hair color. I was very excited to see him, but red flags just kept popping up.

I had also met a young man named Jason. He was extremely good-looking. At first I could not choose between the man who was my age and the younger man. I only liked to date one man at a time. I had never gone out with two men at once. But I figured I would until I had made up my mind.

As for David, we had great sex; he was very into my body. He had the perfect sized dick and knew what to do with it. I hadn't had any orgasms, though. Not many men could give me one. Oh well. If we dated long enough, I would work on it.

I had only been seeing David for three months, and it was already quite the roller-coaster ride. David told me what I wanted to hear. He painted a picture of the life that I wanted, back like the life I'd had with Rudy—the traveling; the nice, big home; getting dressed up for all the social events he had to go to. I loved that life. I was so excited to be talking again and to have that life with David. We had sex every night—well Monday through Friday, but never on Sunday or Saturday. And our liaisons weren't exactly at night either, when it came down to it; they occurred only between 4:00 p.m. and 8:00 p.m. David called me every day five or six times so enthused to talk and to get together.

I believed that he was just really into me. Isn't that how you would see it? We would get together from 4:00 p.m. to 8:30 p.m. We'd have a bite to eat or a drink or two, go back to my place, and fuck. Then he would leave. What was wrong with this picture?

We would make a date for Friday or Saturday, and he would cancel. We would have a weekend planned, and he would cancel. He always canceled on the weekends. One time, his dog had diarrhea, and he could not make it. Another time, there was a mudslide in the back of his house. He had to stay to make sure things would be all right. Always, he had so much drama. Sometimes, he would just say he had made plans before we got together and had to keep them. Those plans just happened to be on our weekends.

One Friday night, he had planned to stay at my place. He got to my house, and we decided to have Chinese food. He would pay if I would pick the order up. Was I just so gullible that I would trust everything a guy said? I really wanted to believe they were honest and truthful.

Well, David got comfortable, and I left to go get the Chinese food. I know now that he probably had to call his wife to tell her he was at his hotel and all checked in. He never invited me to his house.

I would suggest that we go to his place for a weekend, saying that it was time that I saw where he lived. He was supposed to have a very nice home with horses. He always told me we'd go there some other time.

I would get to the point where I'd just had enough and would end things with David. But he would call and say that he was not married; I always believed he was.

I went the library to check and see if he was divorced. I could only find a record of his marriage, but no records of a divorce seemed to exit. I never found his address either. I really wanted to find it or follow him after he got off work to see where he lived. I never did. A friend of mine who lived in my apartment complex, a woman who used to be a man, said we could follow him and she would go to the door and ask for him. Her pickup was too noticeable, and so was my car!

David asked me out for New Year's Eve. I was so excited. We had met the first of November. It had been a yo-yo of a ride, but he wanted to be with me. The day before our date came, and I was ready. I got a call from David. He said, "You are going to be mad at me, but this could not be helped." His dad, who lived in Minnesota, where David had said he'd been the previous week, was in the hospital and would be going in for heart surgery on Sunday. David wouldn't be leaving until late Saturday afternoon, but we still could get together for a few hours.

Was I that good in bed? Was he that addicted to me because I always had my legs spread for him? I hung up.

I started crying. I called my daughter, and we made plans to go to City Grill and meet some friends there. I dressed in my favorite dress—a red, sequin, form-fitted number. We arrived at City Grill, and all I could do was stare at the floor. I was so shocked that I had fallen for someone's lies again. That was it. David was married, and I knew it. I had been with too many men, and if I knew one thing, I knew the pattern of a married man.

The next week, David called. He said he was sick but really wanted to see me. He asked if he could come over. We know that he literally wanted to come over at my place. He said he just wanted to have a drink and be with me. I told him I would bring him chicken soup.

Nothing ever got me to his house. What was he hiding? Well, enough was enough. I told him never to call or e-mail me again—ever.

A year later, I received an e-mail from him through the dating site. The message read, "Hi. There you are. It's been so long. How are you doing?"

I just ignored it.

A few years later, he tried again. This time I e-mailed him back. I told him not to e-mail me or contact me. I noted that I didn't email him or bother him and asked him to return the courtesy, adding that the sight of him made me want to puke and that he disgusted me. So far, that has done the trick.

JASON: THE MAN WHO WANTED A SUGAR MOMMA

Now for the younger man. Jason was very good-looking. He had great body and a terrific smile. I just melted when he looked at me. We met a few times while I was trying to decide between the older and the younger. He was fun but simple.

I had surgery—a tummy tuck—so we could not get together for a while. During that period, he went with his family for a month-long vacation in New York. He called me every night.

I believed we were getting close and that he was worried and wanted to make sure I was there for him and not going anywhere. Yes, I was very gullible and vulnerable. We want to believe in people and trust them.

Jason was soon back from his trip, and I was healing just fine. We decided to meet and see how we were together. I kept asking him to take me to dinner, suggesting that we could meet downtown. But he always stood me up when we planned something like that. So we would just talk on the phone and meet for a drink.

Then he said that we needed to go to my place if we were going to date; we needed to know if we connected. I asked him if he was talking about sex. He said yes, and I jumped right into that one. Sex was right up my alley. So back to my place we went. We made out on my bed, and he started to put his dick inside me, but he got soft. He just couldn't do it. He said he was not over the hurt from his former girlfriend and asked me to give him time.

When he left, I realized that something was wrong again. I just couldn't pinpoint what it was. We weren't really dating or going out; we were just talking and having a drink now and then.

Then there it was. He called and we were having a great time talking like we always did. Suddenly, he said that he did not want me to spend any money until he could help me with it. He wanted to make sure I was putting it in the right places. I could not believe what I was hearing. He was looking for a sugar mama!

That was a wake-up call. I told him that there'd been a guy before him who had gotten all my money and that whatever money I did have was in a trust and would go to my kids.

Jason denied that he wanted a sugar mama. He said he had his own money and made good money. I did not believe him; he was using his cute smile to get me and maybe other women. I told him to go away and never to call me again.

A few months later, I answered a knock on my door without thinking anything of it. There was Jason at my door. I slammed the door in his face. He kept knocking until I opened the door again. He said he wanted to come in. I told him to go away. He had his dog in his car. I went and looked at him. I said, "Now go away and leave me alone."

He just kept smiling.

"Do you think you will get your way just because you are smiling at me with that great smile of yours?" I asked.

He said he usually did. Well, not this time. I told him again to go away and leave me alone and said that, next time, I would call the police. I closed the door, and he drove off.

I did not hear from him for a few weeks or so. I thought he was gone for good. No such luck. Jason started e-mailing me and trying to trick me into seeing him. He called me every week for two years. Sometimes he would just say hi, and sometimes he would try to get me to meet him for dinner. If I agreed, he would stand me up and just want to come to my house. He would get busy at work and only have time to come to my house to see me. We never had a date. What was with that?

Oh well, he was sick. And I was sick to even now and then agree to talk to him during that first year. I soon knew the times he would call—Fridays and on his lunch hour throughout the week—and his phone number by heart. So I would just ignore his calls or hang up on him.

After two years, I got tired of the harassment. Jason called my cell when I was with Bob, a new boyfriend, and I decided to call back when I knew he would not answer and say what I needed to say in front of Bob on his voice mail. That way I would have a witness in case something happened. I told Jason that, if he ever called me again, I would go to his house and break both his legs with a baseball bat. I warned him not to underestimate me; I had done this before and would do it again if he called just one more time. I told him to take my word on this and hung up.

I did not hear from him again. Sometimes we have to take matters into our own hands. Our system is not for the people, and I could have been dead before the police did anything about Jason's harassment. The saga with Jason was finally done, and I was relieved. I have not heard from him since.

PAUL: THE DATING SITE AGAIN

I met another man younger who had a son. I just wanted to date. Paul was nice-looking and nice. We met and started to date. He was on a mission to find a wife.

We went on a few dates and, yes, to bed. He was good and knew how to take care of a woman. His cock was just right for my cunt and mouth. I loved sixty-nine.

Paul was another man who said that a woman should take care of her man two times a day and whenever he needed it.

For our first real dinner date, I entered the room and was seated at a table, and there were flowers and chocolate. Paul looked so handsome. What a nice surprise to be wined and dined to the hilt. I felt so special; he wanted me to commit to him.

We started talking about being together. He had a twelve-year-old son and a nice house we could live in. I was not looking for that situation. And when Paul said that a woman was obligated to take care of her man two times a day, I was turned off. I probably would have done exactly that, but I didn't intend to be told to. I thought he was a little controlling for me. I ended our relationship.

MEN NUMBERS SIXTY-NINE THROUGH NINETY

If you've been counting, you'll know I'm up to about man number sixty-eight by now. There were many others—too many to mention—in parking lots and elevators, in their cars or mine, on the hood of a car, on the beach, in the water. I would put my trench coat on and show up at a boyfriend's place just to fuck. I had so many men I don't remember all their names.

As we know, this is life; this is the way to feel. If a man looked at me, I figured he must like me. Right. Sure, I was always desired when it came to having sex, but to date … What was wrong? I just gave off the scent I guess.

I never did catch any sexual diseases. I was lucky.

What a long learning process life is. Years later, I would wake up to what was real and what was not. I should be thankful I did; I hear some people never do.

CHAPTER FIFTEEN

THE YACHT

BOB NUMBER ONE: IT'S ALL ABOUT BOB, 2007–2009

I MENTIONED BOB EARLIER IN THE book. I had met him twenty-seven years earlier when I'd worked for him. What a dog he'd been, money or not. Even though I had gotten together with him a few times to have a drink, I had never gone to bed with him. For one, he would always call while he was married, and I would never go to bed with a man if I knew he was married. With Bob, he'd call and I wouldn't know he was married again until we'd meet, at which point he'd admit that he did have a wife. In addition, his breath was always bad.

Bob was fun to talk to, though. Back then, that was really all we did, believe it or not. Yes, he had lots of money and was fun. But we still never had sex; that's what made us different.

Now I was on Match.com. I'd found four men on the site who I thought I would go out with and see what they were all about and what might happen. I was on a mission to find my own man.

Then I heard that Bob's third wife had passed away. He had been married to Judy for six years and had also known her for twenty-seven years. I thought about how we had never dated and how he had always wanted to date me and figured why not. I sent him a condolence card.

Two weeks later, he called, and yes, he wanted to meet. He was in Arizona and would be back in two weeks. He asked if I would like to meet, and I agreed. It made him number five on my list. I wanted to find someone to date, and I had never dated him before. I figured, who knew what would happen.

Bob called and invited be to a goldfish contest at his bowling alley in Gresham. He suggested that we meet for a drink in Tualatin and then head over there. I thought it sounded like fun.

That was our first date, and we had a great time. That evening, he took me home, and we were sitting on my couch laughing. He asked why I had gotten in touch with him. I answered that we had never dated and that I thought we might give it a try after all these years. He took that as a great all right, ran up the stairs skipping every other step, jumped into bed, and never left.

It was fun and nice having him there. He was a joker and had a great personality. I thought that was just what I need at the time.

He left the next morning and came back the next night and the next. I wasn't sure what was happening. I wanted to date, but he was there and wanted me to do everything with him. I was a little overwhelmed and surprised. I did not like to be around anyone 24-7.

Bob was so much fun, but the sex—as you know, we need to talk about that—was not good. His cock was small, and he lasted about thirty seconds two times a day. Wow, I got one minute a day. The kissing wasn't there either. He just jumped on and went down on me for a few seconds, just enough to tease and let me know I hadn't been left out of the play. He acted as if it had been a while and that was why he, literally, had shortcomings.

I was having fun, so I decided to let the sex issue go. I had what I thought was a good boyfriend, and we had so much fun together. Later, we could work on the sex and learn what each other needed, just like in any healthy relationship.

One night, we were out to dinner, laughing and enjoying each other. He asked why, if we had so much fun together, we hadn't ever dated or gotten together before. I said I knew why, but he couldn't figure out what I meant. I asked if he want to hear why, and he said he did, as it didn't make sense that we hadn't gotten together earlier. I reminded him that he'd called me through all of his wives and asked me out and that did not work for me. That was not a person I wanted to be with. He was shocked and claimed that he hadn't done that.

When I gave him specific examples, he said that I was referring to things that had happened in his wild days of being a playboy. He assured me that was not him now. He said that he felt good about himself, that he had stood by his wife, and that he had been faithful to her. I told him that was why I was here dating him now. I believed that he had been true to his wife and that he had a heart now and had grown out of his unfaithful past.

He was happy and assured me again that his womanizing was a thing of the past. That made me happy. Again I figured, why not give us a try?

Bob and I had fun. He invited me to everything he did, including his store's functions. He invited me to go with him to the Columbia River Yacht Club. But he let me know that people might be hurtful because they had all known his former wife and had been close to her.

We had started dating in November, and his wife had passed away in September. She had been sick and passing for two years. I guess that enough time had passed for him.

Bob had something going all the time. Every night, he wanted to go out to dinner or meet on the boat and entertain.

December came and, with it, lots of parties to go to. Bob asked me to all of them. The people I met at these festivities were all nice. I found that I already knew some of them from being social out and about.

The yacht club parties were coming up, and he wanted me to go to them. But again he warned me that some people might be rude and standoffish because of Judy.

The Christmas Dinner was very nice, and I was treated nicely. Then there was the New Year's Eve party. I wore my form-fitted, red, sequin dress. I did look hot, and the outfit went over well. We had so much fun.

As Bob had predicted, some people were standoffish, and others were just plain rude. Bob and I were sitting at a table with three other couples, and a girl came up and put her arms around Bob and kissed him on the neck. I had met her a few years earlier, and I knew that she was not a nice younger person. We'd had it out when she took the guy I was seeing at that time. That kind of thing did not go over well with me. Now she was acting like there was or could be something between her and Bob.

I knew better. She was flirty, and Bob just shrugged it off. I acted as if I could care less; she meant nothing. We went about the night and interacted with so many nice people. For the most part, the club members really welcomed me.

Then came the end of the night. As I was waiting for Bob by the door, one of the women members came up to me and said that she hoped I'd had fun. She added that she probably wouldn't see me again, "as we know Bob; he goes through women," and I was probably just for the night. She was friends with the younger girl who had come up and hugged Bob in a sexual way, and I let her know she was not wanted and that she should go away. I was sure the two women had gotten together to hurt me. Bob could not believe it.

Bob was so attentive and thoughtful. He was always a gentleman.

Everyone liked him. He was the top of everyone's list for making the party fun. I met so many people through the yacht club and his store gatherings. Everyone treated me well.

One person from the yacht club came up and said that he had never seen Bob so happy, that I was good for him.

I had worked at Thriftway for Bob twenty-seven years earlier and knew a few of his top men who had been with him at least that long. They all treated me very well and with respect. One of the men who had been with him for thirty years was familiar to me. I had known him back in my checking years when he ran the store, and I hadn't liked him then. He'd be a tall, skinny, arrogant kid. I ran into him at one of the parties, and I was surprised to see that he had grown up to be a nice-looking man. He'd filled out and had a beautiful, nice wife and two blond little girls.

We hit it off. I enjoyed talking to him. He was not working at this time. A drunk driver had hit his car and he had suffered some kind of brain damage. The accident may have cut his life short. He did do well and said that, if I ever wanted to talk, he had stories to tell on Bob and would be happy to fill me in.

I already had an idea. I just hoped he had changed and had grown up at age sixty-eight.

Bob had a home in Arizona, and we would fly there. His former in-laws lived there and, of course, wanted to meet me. The family took to me and liked me, but Judy's sister had a lot of questions for me. She wanted to know how long I had known Bob, given that it had only been a few months since Judy had passed when we started dating. The conversation went well; I guess we answered all the questions she had.

As in Oregon, I had a lot of fun with everyone Bob knew in Arizona. We all went to dinners and had dinner parties.

In February, my birthday month, Bob put on a party for me at one of his friend's bar in north Portland. Lots of people from the yacht club, along with my friends, came.

Bob had a cake brought in, but it was not for me. He brought it for the wife or the bar owner; it was her favorite cake. The deliverers took it in the back. I had no cake for my birthday, and that, believe it or not, was the start of a new set of red flags. I would have ordered a cake for my sixtieth birthday if I had known I would not have one.

Bob and I had stopped on our way to the party to have a drink downtown, and we had two cars. We decided to take my Jeep. Bob got in to drive, and he'd already had a little too much to drink. As he was backing out of the parking space, he took off my side mirror and bent my bumper. We went on to the party and had a lot of fun.

The next day I mentioned that I needed to go have my Jeep looked at. Bob just said, "Oh, yeah, you do."

I took it in to be fixed, and the bill came to five hundred dollars. When I told Bob, he did not offer to pay. I asked, "Are you going to pay for it? After all, you did it."

He said he would, but when the bill came, I paid it. Again, I had to ask Bob to pay. He did give me the money, but it was like pulling teeth. This was another red flag. I wasn't complaining, but Bob was supposed to be a millionaire, and I worked hard for what money I made. Plus, it was only polite to offer to pay for what he did.

Around the end of February, Bob started saying that I should move in with him. On the fifth of July, he would be going up north with about thirty other yachts, first to Roach Harbor for about four days and then farther north. They would stay until the first of August and then come back down the river. The trip sounded very good, but I ignored him about moving in. I did not want to live with him or move. I had a comfortable place to live and a nice job. I felt I was just where I needed to be and did not want to change my situation.

As we know, Bob had cheated on three wives; he'd always called me even though he was married. I wanted him as a friend and buddy to party with and date but nothing more. I did not care what he had. I did not feel good inside about moving in with him. The subject made me uncomfortable. I ignored him every time he brought it up and simply changed the subject. I knew I was going to have to answer him at some point.

Bob's right-hand man on the boat was a good friend of his. The two men had known each other for seventeen years. Well, Peter and I became friends. He told me that, if I did not move in with Bob and go with him on the two-month trip, it would be over between us. Bob would find someone else. He explained that this was what Bob wanted and I really had no choice if I wanted to keep dating Bob.

Again, I went against the voice inside of me. Bob and I were having so much fun. I decided to answer him the next time he brought up the subject of my moving in. I had so many questions to ask and so much I wanted to talk to him about. When he mentioned me living with him, I said yes, living together would be so much fun. I told him that I had so much we needed to talk about. He just shrugged off the latter part and said, "Great! Let's plan it."

He told me that he would have some of his men with a truck move me and that he would take care of all the expenses. Okay, that was great. As we know, he could afford it.

I gave the company I was managing for a sixty-day notice. I had so much furniture that I loved. Where would we put it? At first, Bob agreed to pay for storage, and then he said we could put it in the garage. I was thinking, *This is life; we're not playing games here. We are going to make it as a couple.*

Was I thinking right? I think the answer is obvious.

Oh lord, the story really starts here. And here we go!

Finally, it was time for the trucks to come. I haven't mentioned yet that I had been trying to talk to Bob about my income and my bills for the past sixty days. I wanted him to know what I had coming in and what I needed to pay out and be sure that he realized I couldn't just move in and not pay my bills. This was a normal conversation that should have happened by this point. I had tried and tried, but every time I had mentioned the subject or said we had something we needed to talk about, he had just cut me off. Really, he couldn't care less what I had to say; he just made his own conversation.

Again this was a flag—a giant, bright red one that was waving in the air. But I ignored it. I didn't listen to my inner voice—the part of you that knows better and tells you what you need to hear. But I wasn't listening because I was just going with the flow of Bob. I was focusing on what Bob needed, not what I needed.

I asked Bob if he had the trucks and some men ready for the move. He didn't answer.

I had to move soon. "Bob," I said, "this is the week, and we need to have the movers come."

He told me to just get a truck from the store. I got a truck and started moving some of my things over to his place. I needed a bigger vehicle, so I rented a U-Haul truck and asked if my son and his kids could help and if Bob would pay them to move me. I picked up the truck, and my son came over with his boys. Together, we moved my things out of my apartment and into Bob's garage.

I gave my nice, big bed with a pillow top that was the best to sleep on to my son. The mattress alone had cost me two thousand dollars. My son took my white sectional that was worth three thousand dollars new. I had some nice things, but where was I going to put them? Bob had everything. He had two homes and a seventy-two-foot yacht with four bedrooms. We did not need my things. So my son gave my sectional to his girlfriend. He sold the rest at a garage sale or gave stuff to people who needed it.

As you see, the storage unit did not come through, and now I was paying for the move.

Yes, our inner voices know the truth, but we don't listen. You would think that, by now—with all the men, all the self-help books, all the deceit I'd faced, and all the physics' counseling—I would have learned. I had seen so many red flags, and yet, I was moving in.

I told Bob that I need money to pay my son for his help and to pay for the U-Haul truck. We took the truck back, and getting him to pay for the rental was like pulling teeth. I gave my son a hundred dollars; he didn't want to take it, but he did.

Now come the juicy parts, and bad just kept getting worse. I know I am not an idiot. Did I just want to trust that people were honest and giving and real and motivated by their hearts? Did I just want to believe that love was real and that I could feel good and find honesty? We all want to believe this. I wanted to!

I was unpacking and feeling somewhat excited. I wasn't sure what to expect. Bob walked into the kitchen, and we started talking. I said, "You know, Bob, this is for real. It is not a game to me. This is for life."

He shrugged his shoulders and said, "Yeah, of course," and walked off. Here was another red flag.

Peter, who lived on Bob's yacht and had a room in the house when he was in town, came in while I was unpacking. He said that he wanted to talk to me. He had known Bob for seventeen years, and he wanted share with me, in confidence, how proud he was of Bob.

Peter explained that Bob had two women friends he had been seeing while he was with Judy. I was fuming inside, but I didn't let Peter see my feelings. I acted like I was just very interested in what he was saying, and I was very interested. Peter said that one of the women had thought she would be moving into the house as soon as Judy passed away. The other was hoping the same. Bob took the one woman out to a nice dinner and let her know that he was with me and that he would not be getting together with her anymore. He really wanted to make this work with me.

I was somewhat flattered, but I had caught him in a lie. Bob had said more than once that he felt good about himself because he had been there for Judy and that he had not been involved with anyone else.

Apparently, Bob had just called the other woman and told her about me.

The next few months were good. I filled my time with moving in and trying to keep up with Bob and his nightly entertaining. I moved some of my stuff onto the boat, so I had a wardrobe there and at the house in Arizona. It felt like too much fun; what a life. Bob and I always held hands in the beginning; we danced around like two kids having fun.

Bob and I were at the yacht club three nights a week. There were parties every week, and he was the center of attention. We all took the yachts out together frequently. I went along on the two-month trip up north, and we got along great then. Life was grand and full. I never cooked. Bob wanted to go out for dinner every night. We entertained on the boat and always had someone around.

Bob liked sharing what he had to show off. Men loved him. He always wanted me to wear something sexy on the boat so he could show me off to his friends at the Columbia Yacht Club. I did not. That wouldn't have gone over well with everyone, and I liked the wives.

We flew to Arizona once a month and entertained there too. I was really tired, and I wanted some private time. But that did not happen.

We went to Hawaii with a group from all of the Thriftway grocery stores. The Resers of Reser's Foods were friends of Bob's, and they were very nice. The wife knew what I was in for, and it was nice to have someone I could relate to.

I met at least five hundred friends of Bob's; all of them were nice. Peter and Michelle sold their dot-com for $35 million.

One night at a dinner party at the yacht club, Pete came over, and we talked. He was a nice-looking guy. He said, "I know you are monogamous, but if you ever want to just have sex with another man, I would like to be on your list."

I assured him he would be first.

We met lots of swingers at the club, but we did not go there.

In May, Bob planned our trip to Arizona. We would fly there and drive back. He wanted to bring back a car he had there so that we'd to have it here. That would give us four cars, three of Bob's and mine. The road trip was a vacation from hell. We flew in, and of course he had a party planned, as always. Every time we landed, we went to the grocery store to buy food for a dinner party. He would never tell me about the plans. I just was there—a body. The dinner parties were always so nice and fun. Bob's in-laws, Judy's family, would be there. I really liked them, and they liked me too.

We took off on our road trip in his Magnum. We took seven days to get from Phoenix, Arizona, to Portland, Oregon. During this trip from hell, all the red flags I'd ignored came out in full color. During the entire car trip, he did not speak to me at all. I would try to talk or ask a question, and he would ignore me. After having tried fifty times to talk with no response from him, I finally decided not to insult myself anymore. I would just get home and leave. This was enough!

I decided to read or make calls and schedule appointments for when I get home. As soon as I opened a paper and started to read or got on the phone, Bob would knock me on the arm and push at me for my attention. He would say, "Listen to this" and point to the radio. It was always sports. "Listen," he would say, pushing me on the shoulder and totally interrupting me.

Finally, I just sat there and looked out the window until we got home. He wanted control of my time.

We did have nice dinners out at night after we'd stop and check in at a hotel. But even then, Bob's behavior left much to be desired.

One time, we went to get a drink. The waitress asked me what I wanted, and when I started to answer, Bob leaned back and said, "It doesn't matter what she wants. I know what I want."

The waitress looked at me and then back at Bob and took his drink order. When she turned her attention back to me, I said, "As I was saying before we were so rudely interrupted, I would like a glass of wine."

Bob's rudeness just continued. We walked on the beach, and he looked at every woman as if she was naked. He had a big tummy and man boobs—gross. Women did not look at him. I was slim, had a small waist, and looked good, but he insulted me as we walked as if I were nothing. Where did I find these toads?

When we were in our hotel rooms, he would watch sports as if I was not there—except when he wanted sex. Then he would be cutesy. Come on; you've got to be kidding. I had to, but I didn't want to go there. He just grossed me out.

Once, we packed and left the room. Bob, who had only a backpack, opened the door and went out, letting it shut in my face. I was pulling a suitcase and had a shoulder bag and my purse.

I could not wait until we got home. I had to be patient. I wanted out so badly. Wouldn't you? Money or not, Bob was a complete chauvinist; it was all about Bob.

We would be driving through Sunset Beach, California, where a very good friend of mine lived. I knew I would be able to see her building from the freeway, and I wanted to stop for just a few minutes to leave a message on her door. I knew she wasn't currently living in the building, so the stop wouldn't take long. I wasn't even 100 percent sure she still owned the building, as I had lost track of her a few years earlier. Stopping by would be perfect.

I kept my eye out, and there it was. Bob just kept on driving; he told me to call her after we'd left town.

What a rude, thoughtless bastard. Stopping to leave a note for my friend was the only thing I had asked to do during our entire road trip.

We got home, and it was obvious that I was upset. Bob wanted to talk. I did not want to talk to him. I told him I needed to rest and regroup. Then I would talk to him.

After a few days, I told him I was ready to talk. I laid everything on him. I pointed out how badly he was mistreating me and said that, if I had known he was like this, I would not have moved in at all. I told him I had a list of fifty things he'd done wrong and that every move he made was so insulting to me. I just wanted to get out and away from him.

I guess because of his money he was shocked that I was not willing to be available on his time and dime. I was a body to him—I could be any body—not a mate. One time, I had a doctor's appointment, and I'd had to change it three times to accommodate his schedule. Another time, I was going to fly to Canada and meet him on a Tuesday. He wanted me to go on Monday with him. I had an appointment with my psychiatrist, but Bob told me to cancel and go with him. I called and canceled while we were driving to the airport, and he gave me his visa card to cover the two hundred dollars charge for the canceled appointment. His dime, his time.

He wanted us to make it and to try again. I said, "Okay, let's see."

Things were good for a few months. He made some changes. He opened the doors for me. He tried to remember to make me a drink first before making one for his friends, an improvement since mine was normally last, if he didn't just tell me to make my own.

How things change when one moves in. Men talk about women changing after a couple moves in together. Not this time. Bob did a whole turnaround. He went from nice to asshole!

Well, the changes couldn't last. Bob's voice started changing, and he started leaving the house without saying he was leaving. I would call his phone, and he would say that he'd called to me. Sure he had. I hadn't lost my hearing. All the little things added up to one obvious truth. He was playing around again. That was Bob; everyone who knew Bob knew he was a player. Bob had bad hygiene and bad breath. He ate with his mouth open and food would fall out of his mouth. I would wipe his mouth. He had the worst manners. He didn't care. He was Bob.

I took all his underwear from both homes and the yacht, threw them away, and bought new ones. The old ones looked like he'd shit in them. There was no way I could get turned on knowing how bad his hygiene was.

In December, I went out with the girls and met Larry. How refreshing—someone nice to look at who was talking to me.

I am going to finish with Bob and then write about Larry. I want this story over with. Telling it is draining. I knew I was going to leave. I wanted to plan for March. I had to plan and find both work and a place to live.

During the first week in December, Bob was sitting in his office chair and heard me upstairs. He asked me to come into his office. He had a cocky, arrogant attitude.

He asked what I wanted for Christmas. I said I wanted a ring and added that I had been working out, so I wanted it heavy—three karats. Bob said that he never wanted to marry again; marriage did not work for him. I replied that I did not want to marry him; I had told him before not to ask me to marry him. I was not interested in getting married. I was simply a body at his beck and call. Instead, I wanted to put him on the spot and play his game. I said I just wanted a commitment ring, nothing more.

"Oh," he said.

One of the yacht club members, Eric, owned a jewelry store, and he held an annual Christmas men's night at the store. To continue with my plan, I called Eric and said that it would be great if, while Bob was at the function, he would show Bob some three karat diamonds. Eric loved the idea. I put Bob on the spot in front of all the guys from the yacht club.

A few weeks later, Bob started acting so cutesy. He started making jokes with me about Christmas. I knew he had bought a ring. I also went to a psychic, who confirmed my suspicion.

Christmas arrived, and Bob could not wait to give me the ring. He did get me a two and a half karat ring; it was beautiful. The ring held a $15,000 diamond. The jewelry store had overcharged him, but that was okay. I loved the ring. He had also gotten me a $500 charm bracelet with my two doggies on it. Now stop thinking, *Oh what a great guy*. This does not make him a nice guy; get real.

All of a sudden, he started introducing me as his wife or his fiancée. We were talking on the phone, and he was in Arizona. He told me that he had told his in-laws that I was his fiancée.

I just came unglued. I said, "Wait, that is not right." Bob knew how I felt, and we had not talked about getting engaged. He just said that we would talk when he got home and settle this with plans to be married.

I didn't think so.

He got home, and he was still introducing me as his wife or fiancée. I told myself I would not marry him but I would not move out in March either. I would give this relationship another try, again. January and February were good, I guess.

February came, and it was Valentines' Day. I decided to surprise Bob when he got home. I had a bubble bath ready, with candles, champagne, and chocolate strawberries. It would be a gift for him and for me. We had a spiral staircase that led to the second floor from the front door. I put a trail of silk red rose petals from the front door leading up the stairs to the tub. I was wearing a sheer teddy and come fuck me heels. I heard Bob drive up. I stood above on the landing waiting. I knew no one had ever done this for him before for him.

He came in the door and looked up and he said, "Wow." He headed up the stairs, but when he got to the top, he turned to the right of me and said, "I will be right there." He headed into his office, I guess to check his e-mails. Yes, it was all about Bob. This did not matter to him.

Finally, he came in and we got into the tub. We were laughing and joking sexually. He was surprised and thanked me.

I said, "Bob, in order for us to make it, I need more from you sexually."

I had told my doctor about him, and she mentioned a spa in Arizona where couples could go to experiment with each other. I mentioned that I would like to try the spa, and he said okay. We know he could afford it, right. I continued, telling him that I needed more foreplay and wanted to have orgasms.

My friends coached me to teach him like one does with a new lover—to show him what I wanted. I always did with others, but Bob was different than a hundred other guys. Everything is what he wants to do and how he wants to do it; there was no changing his ways. That was it.

I thought the spa could be good. We never went, though I tried to make it happen.

We had a good evening. He of course told all the men at the yacht club about my Valentine's surprise. Now we know what they were thinking. They wanted me; the men were looking at me sexually, and their wives could tell.

I had fun of course, but I was always on my toes, listening to what Bob said and watching what he did. I had caught him in so many lies—downright lies. I won't even get into that.

I did have a lot of fun with all the yacht club members, the boating, and the parties. This was a good life, except for I had a partner who was not monogamous and I was just a body. No matter how much money Bob had I couldn't feel good about being with someone who treated me like this.

One night I was in bed and Bob came to bed around 10:00 p.m. I just looked up and asked if he had taken a shower. He was excited and said, "Oh."

I said, "No, not for sex." I just wanted him to shower.

He got into bed, and my mouth just blurted out, "I am so unhappy. I cannot do this anymore."

He just said, "What?"

"I feel I have no self-worth," I told him. "This is no way to feel or live."

He instantly started talking about how we could be so happy and had so much to do together. He started to ask why, but then he caught himself.

The next morning, Bob said he would stay on the boat and give us some time apart. We agreed that we would not say anything to anyone for a few days. This was Monday. On Tuesday morning, Bob called and said he'd thought about our situation, and he felt I should start dating other men. Just like that. This was his way of saying he was now going to publicly be with other women. This gave him an excuse.

The next week, a dinner party was scheduled at the yacht club on Thursday. I decided not to go and went out with a girlfriend in downtown Portland instead. The next morning, I went to the club to have breakfast with everyone, and one of my friends, the owner of an eighty-eight-foot yacht, came up to me as I walked in and said, "Heads up. Bob had a date last night."

I could feel the coldness in the room. I sat with Bob and our friends. Everything felt different, as if we didn't even know each other. Of course, Bob told everyone he ended it, to save face I guess.

My son said, "Well, Mom, he had never been dumped before."

Bob had had a date the first week I told him I wanted to part. I hadn't even moved out yet. That he had been seeing her before I even told him I wanted to end our relationship was so obvious it made me sick. Yes, I would get past his betrayal, but it took a while to process how hurtful the kind of abuse I had taken from Bob was. I was able to do so and to move on in a healthier way.

Bob had the money, and all my friends with whom I'd spent so much time—we'd gotten together several times a week and had traveled together—just shrugged me off. I told Bob that, if he bad-mouthed me, I would send a letter about him and the fifty things I had to say about him. Now I had a list of one hundred things that he had done to me.

I told him I would be moved out in August, which was three months away. It would take me that long to get a job and the furnishings I would need to move.

We met at one point. I gave him a letter I wanted him to sign, saying he would not ask for anything back—not the ring, not the visa he had given me to use. He wanted his attorney to look at this letter. That was fine.

His attorney said that he should rewrite the letter in his words and he thought that would be good. As you will see, I wrote the letter to cover myself. I was not going to walk out with everything I'd worked for gone. I didn't want anything extra at all. I just wanted what I'd come in with. When Bob came back with the letter, I wanted it notarized and signed. He did not want to do this, but I insisted, and he did.

Meanwhile, we arranged to meet at a coffee shop. I asked him for the thousand dollars he usually gave me in the middle of the month to pay my bills. He said no. I told him I had no way to live. I wasn't working, and we still lived together. He shrugged his shoulders.

I asked him to help me financially with the move and to help me get new furniture, since I had given all of mine away when I moved in. He said I could take some things from the garage for the yacht. I said, "What? Everything there is old and moldy." He thought I could have a few things in the house, like the bed in the guest room.

As I walked away, I thought to myself, *No. I will not walk away and lose again.* How dare he? He was a millionaire and had just told me to move out without anything.

LEAVING BOB

My mind went to work. I had to take care of myself. I went straight to the bank and withdrew a thousand dollars off his visa, which was mine to use as I wanted. I started calling all my creditors and paid off my bills with the visa. I could not afford the bills on my own, and by paying off these debts, I saved myself a thousand a month.

I asked the bank to up the limit, and they did. I was on the account, but it was Bob's responsibility to pay the debt, not mine. I gave myself some money to move out as well. Why not?

I wanted to buy a Mercedes that Bob had. The car had belonged to Judy, and he was trying to sell it. I talked him down from $9,000 to $3,500, since I had from him a list of things that needed done. I paid for the car with a money order. I don't feel I am dishonest, but I paid him with his own money that I had withdrawn from the visa. I also had him sign a bill of sale. He could not understand all this legal signing, but I knew I needed to cover my butt.

On July 5, 2008, Bob left in the yacht for Canada as he did every year. I moved out July 6, 2008. Bob thought I was staying in the house. He wanted me to send him his mail. I did, but I kept out the envelope that contained the visa account, so he did not have the statement for July. He would not know what he owed on it until August. That was good.

I took whatever I needed from the house and furnished my apartment quite nicely. I took the bed from our guest room and the mattress from our bed. I took the kitchen table but not the nice dining table. He told everyone at the yacht club that I took everything in the house. Oh well.

I moved to a nice place, not too far from the house we'd lived in. He did not know that I had gotten a post office box two months before I moved.

Well, I had dealt with more drama than I cared to. But I had moved. I was free and no longer owned or controlled. I was not on his time and his dime, Scheduled twenty-four hours a day. I could do what I wanted, and I could think for myself. I found that I just wanted to enjoy my quiet time and work out. I did not want to date; I just wanted to breathe and enjoy family and friends. I didn't care to be busy, since we had been going out every night for so long. I just wanted to be home.

Bob got the visa bill, and all hell broke loose. I did not care. I heard from his attorney, who was a friend. The attorney made it clear that he was writing the letter for Bob, that these were not his words, and that he did not believe what was being said. Bob threatened to put me in jail for fraud, stealing his money, and charging on his visa.

His visa? He had given me the visa to use and had my name on the account.

I closed the visa. I know I had done everything by the book. I beat him at his own game. How dare he use me as if I was a body? The whole thing was over and done. I got an attorney, and he said that Bob had more money than I did, so I should give him back what he asked for. Several of the yacht club wives had used this attorney before and referred me to him. He thought he knew Bob. I knew him better. Justice did not happen often, but it did here.

Still, the hurt didn't go away just because one proved a point.

I did not and could not date for three and a half years after ending things with Bob. I just could not go there. My entire experience with Bob was very draining. I had shut down inside. I did not desire sex or a partner. I just existed.

We all go through so much. Dating is work, and it should be fun and honest. But that isn't always the case.

CHAPTER SIXTEEN

MT. PARK:
MY APARTMENT ON THE HILL

MT. PARK, JULY 2008–2009

I MOVED INTO A BEAUTIFUL APARTMENT in a parkway in the Mt. Park area. It was situated right on top of the hill overlooking where Bob and I had shared a house. I got a post office box address so Bob would not know where I was living or that I was living as well as I was.

The apartment was lovely. It had two bedrooms, two bathrooms, a fireplace, and a full wall of top-to-bottom windows looking out on green grass and a patio. I had a garage that I could walk out to from my apartment as well, which made for a great storage area.

I was so happy to be back on my own. I could make up my own mind, and no one was scheduling me 24-7. I could go out if I wanted to or just stay in. I had no boss, no one making me party every night.

I could make my own decisions. I did not want to date at all. After Bob and being treated like a body instead of a person, I just wanted my freedom. I would go out but not very often. I had a hard time leaving my home. I just wanted to be with myself, not obligated to anyone for anything. I didn't want to have to give anyone sex or think about pleasing someone else.

I loved my apartment. I lived in it for a year, until my savings was going to run out. I needed to look for another job as an apartment manager so that I wouldn't have to pay rent and would have an income as well.

LARRY NUMBER TWO: TALL, GOOD-LOOKING, AND NICE (HMMM?)

I was still with Bob when I first met Larry. I went out with the girls on December 7, 2007, and he and I met at the Portland City Grill downtown. We always sat at the bar on the barstools at the end of the bar next to the piano. That way, we could listen to the music, watch the piano player, and look at the view out the big windows.

That night, some of the girls went and sat at a table, and a few of us stayed at the bar. A very nice-looking man was sitting a few stools down from me. I was ignoring him. A girlfriend of mine, Bonnie, leaned over to talk to him. Why not? He looked pretty good, better than anyone else there for sure. Bonnie started up a conversation with him, and we had a few things in common. I started talking a little.

Bonnie went to sit with the other girls, but I wanted to stay in my favorite spot now that I was enjoying talking to this guy. I just wanted to talk. I never really had conversations with Bob. (Heaven forbid someone else might have something to say around him that was not about him.) So I was enjoying this new guy and laughing, and I liked looking at him. I told him my situation, adding that I planned to move out in March once I'd gotten myself together and my ducks in a row. I shared with him that the person I was with did not know that I was planning this.

Larry asked if we could at least get together for a cup of coffee. That was a hard one. He was so good-looking, and he seemed nice. I was still living with someone, though I was unhappy. I said yes, and we had a terrific time together. We made a dinner date and then another.

We were having dinner at Manzoni's in Lake Oswego and decided to have one drink afterward, so we went into the bar. We ordered Spanish coffees. I love them. I did not worry about us being seen together. I don't know why. I just didn't.

We were talking, and all of a sudden, Larry said that as much as he liked going out together, he thought we should commit to each other and be a couple.

"What?" I said, surprised. "I am still living with Bob." Not knowing what else to say I added that his suggestion wouldn't work for me. Maybe we could go out some more and see whether or not we were compatible in bed. I already knew his kisses could make my clothes fly off. He had walked me to my car one night and had kissed me good night, and that is what a kiss should be. He was leaning against me, and I could feel how well-endowed he was. Yum. This was my kind of man. I was into that, and good kissing was what I needed. Bob was not a kisser; well he wasn't great at anything else either.

As Larry and I would talk and meet, I started to get the feeling that he wanted a sugar mama.

I parted from Bob on July 6, 2008. Larry and I were still meeting, and we still hadn't been to bed. At one point, he wanted to come over and cook me dinner. I still could not go there. I did not want to be intimate with him. Why not? He was good-looking, and I had always wanted a good-looking man on my arm. He seemed to be nice.

You see, I was starting to listen to my inner voice—that voice we ignore that could guide us in the right direction, the voice that we do not want to listen to, doing instead what we want, right or wrong, the rebellious, wild way.

Why now when he was so good-looking and everything I'd always wanted in bed? Something was wrong with this guy. We were out on the eve of St. Patrick's Day at Jake's Bar downtown. I was there with some girlfriends, Larry was there and looking very good. I thought we might spend some time together, dance and maybe get to know each other better. Well, he was busy, at what I did not know. He said he was spending time with some friends he'd come with.

Then I saw that he was with a group that included one girl, who he said he was with as a friend. That told me a lot. I knew the girl, as I had run into her often in Portland; she was part of many of the same social groups as I was. And I did not like her. We'd had a few run-ins. I thought that, if he liked her, he was not the type of guy I would like.

At one point, I just said to him, "I think you're looking for a sugar mama."

He was kind of secretive at times; I did not know what was going on with him. He never invited me to his home. That was a big flag for me and should be to all of you too. If you don't see where a man lives within the first few weeks, maybe a month, of dating him, something is up. He's married, or he is poor and doesn't want you to see that he has nothing. Or maybe he has a girlfriend he is living with.

Larry denied wanting a sugar mama. He said he made plenty of money and had a lot of assets. He did not need any woman's money. I did not believe this. In the beginning, we agreed to split the bills and take care of our own tabs when we met. He seemed to pay every time we went out. That was nice. Still, I really believed that, knowing the lifestyle I'd had with Bob, Larry thought I had money too and that he could live well too and just service me as a couple. Larry thought that, with or without Bob, I would always live a wealthy life. And he wanted that too.

We finally stopped getting together. He was too complicated, and I was done trying to figure him out. I was growing inside; so many changes were taking place within me that would allow me to move forward in a better way. Little did I know how true this was. I wouldn't discover the truth until down the road, and I'll share that discovery later in the book. I'm saving it for the right time in my story.

PETER, SO NICE AND GOOD-LOOKING: WHY NOT HIM?

I was running around one day just in my workout clothes—Capri tights and a little black top. I was feeling good about how I looked and about my newfound freedom. I decided to go into Stanford's in Lake Oswego and have an appetizer at 5:00 p.m., happy hour time. I usually sat at the bar. I love a bar stool under my ass. I don't know why; I just do. Maybe I think I'm supposed to be happy; it's happy hour, right.

This time, I sat at a little table against the wall facing the bar. Seven little tables for two or four people were arranged in that area. As I was sitting and watching people like I do, I noticed a good-looking guy to the left of me sitting at one of the tables, like me, with his back against the wall. A blond at the table next to him was talking to him. That she was flirting with him was very clear.

I was trying not to make it obvious that I was looking at him. He was so good-looking—tall with a great head of coal black hair and a nice, strong face. Now I noticed he was looking at me and was trying to get my attention. I just kept looking elsewhere, as if I didn't notice him. I ordered my appetizer, and then I looked up. He was getting up and walking toward me. He stopped in front of me and kind of looked at me for a moment before saying, "Hi."

He introduced himself as Peter and asked if I was sitting alone. He wondered if I wanted to sit with him and visit. I was shocked that he wanted to meet me and not be with the two blonds next to him.

We moved my things over to his table and started talking. I found him to be so much fun to talk to and very nice to look at too! He told me that he was in the food business. I had to ask if he knew

Bob—the insult and disaster of my life—who had five grocery stores. My life with Bob had been very adventurous and fun, but it hadn't been a good one because he treats his women with no respect, seeing them as objects.

Peter of course knew Bob through the food industry.

Peter had just moved here from back east. He had been traveling here every other week or more, as Oregon was his home base. He was married, and he and his wife were, after a lot of years together, getting a divorce. I did not know whether to believe this or not. In a bar, "I'm getting a divorce," could be a classic pick-up line.

He seemed honest, but you never knew. Peter and his wife had a lot of assets to split and paperwork to do. He did not want the divorce; she did. And I could tell that he was hurt.

Besides being so good-looking, Peter was a lot of fun to get together with. I thought, *Wow, I leave Bob, and now I am attracting good-looking guys who are nice too.*

I was not ready to go to bed with any man, not even this nice, good-looking man. Yeah, I had been with every asshole in Portland, and now this nice guy, who was good-looking and fun, was in front of me, and I wasn't ready. Peter was honest and told it how it was. He drank a lot of wine and got loud and very talkative. He was six foot five and had a good body. He worked out, and he worked hard. We talked about dating each other, but I just wasn't ready. I don't know exactly how to explain it; I simply wasn't attracted to taking the next step. He kissed well, but I wasn't turned on by his kisses. Or maybe it was just me again. He knew Bob, and I didn't like that.

One night, we were out drinking lots of wine, and we came back to my place. Peter came in and asked if he could stay on the couch; he had had a lot to drink. I was not ready for that at all.

Bob had had a date the first week I told him I wanted to part. I hadn't even moved out yet. That he had been seeing her before I even told him I wanted to end our relationship was so obvious it made me sick. Yes, I would get past his betrayal, but it took a while to process how hurtful the kind of abuse I took from Bob was. I was able to do so and to move on in a healthier way.

I told Peter that he could stay in my bed but asked him, please, no sex or playing at all.

We went to bed, and he was so nice. He just held me. We did make out some, and that was nice too. Because of his height, one would think he might be very well hung. As we lay there, from what I could feel, I believed that he was just a nice size, nothing to be scared about. We slept. That was all.

I had always wanted to have a good-looking man, and now I had two with whom I could get together for dinner or drinks. So why not keep this up? Finally, I had what I wanted in my life. All my life I had wanted to meet good-looking men and be asked out. And now I couldn't go there at all.

Was I finally setting boundaries that I should have had years ago—now that I had these good-looking (and much younger) men asking me out? I knew the feeling I wanted to feel, and I did not want to settle for less than that. And now going to bed and having sex was not the most important thing in my life. Can you believe that came out of my mouth? I had come a long way.

But I did not know where I was or needed to be yet!

Peter could not understand why I wouldn't choose us. He was getting a divorce. He was living here now, and we had so much fun together. So why not?

I just could not. Maybe if he was an asshole like the men I had picked in the past. But no; that wasn't it. Maybe he was too tall or drank too much. No, the truth was I was not really ready. My freedom was so important to me right now.

Peter and I have stayed friends, and I really like having him as my friend. He has a girlfriend, and they live together. She is fine with us being friends. For a while, he would still ask every now and then, "Why not us?" I think this has passed now. I just knew he was not the one. Or was he?

Steve: Fuck Me and Other Women, Oh No!

I got on another Internet dating site. I had thought I would never do this again. For one, I'd had so many problems with online dating in the past. And secondly, I did not like how degrading these sites were to women.

However, a girlfriend of mine wanted me to get on the site to see a picture of a guy she was interested in. In order to look, you have to fill out some information and log into the site. Once I was on, I couldn't help looking to see what fish were out there.

I ran across a profile that made me go, "Wow." I didn't think this guy would get together with me. But I wanted to try anyway. He responded, and was I on a roll? I'd attracted three good-looking men since Bob. Bob may have had money and been fun, but he had a big tummy and man boobs and a little dick, not to mention that he lasted about thirty seconds. He was not for me.

This guy, Steve, and I decided to meet. He lived in Camas, Washington. He worked over here, so we planned to meet at Pete's Coffee in Bridgeport. We parked our cars next to each other and recognized each other from our pictures. We were attracted to each other as soon as we saw each other. We walked and talked and made our way into the coffee shop. We decided to get together on a date.

St. Patrick's Day was coming up in a few days, and he and his friends were getting together and going out someplace downtown. I was going to Jake's with my friends. He suggested that we might try and meet up. We talked on the phone, and I could tell that he wanted to meet again. Then he called and said that his friends had decided to go to Jake's and that he would be there.

I was so excited. No one had caught my attention at all since Bob, and now I was meeting this guy I was attracted to at Jake's. I would be there with my girlfriends, and we'd be seeing all our friends that would be out that night.

We got to Jake's, and there he was with his friends. We started talking and dancing and kissing. I could not help kissing him; he was so delicious. He took my hand and walked me through the place. Women seemed to like him. He stayed focused on me. As we danced, I was getting very turned on, something I hadn't felt in a few years, even after meeting two good-looking men.

Larry and Peter hadn't done anything for me. I don't know why. Was it because they were nice, because they were total gentlemen all the time and did not try to have sex with me on the first date? I don't know. But as Steve and I danced and he paraded me around the place, I just kept getting more and more excited. I was back to my old ways. I wanted him. I looked at him and said, "I'm taking you home. I have to have you."

He did not say no, and of course he'd had the same idea in mind. As for me I wasn't thinking with the right head or mind. My body just took over.

When it was late, we got his car and went back to my place. I thought I'd died and gone to heaven. I was so gaga over this man.

Steve left at 3:00 a.m. He had three kids at home. He told me that his wife had passed away in December. She'd been very sick for two years. He knew he was ready to move on because he'd had two years to think about being single and finding someone. Steve told me he was looking for a girlfriend. He knew he wanted a mate and did not want to be alone.

You know what I was thinking. We'd hit it off, and we were going to bed. This was the man I wanted.

He called the next morning and wanted to come over at lunchtime. I just jumped for that one. He wanted me—to see me. It was me he wanted, right, not just for sex? He wanted to see me. I just wanted him more.

Noon was so good. I just liked looking at him and feeling him and kissing him. Everything felt so good. Yes, we all think of course we will be dating and where will this go. Is this the guy it sure feels right in bed and we are attracted.

I bought two tickets to a play for $120. I mentioned to Steve that he could take me to dinner before the play. He said we could stop on the way and have a bite to eat. I said no, I would like a nice, romantic dinner at the Portland City Grill. He said okay. I knew he could afford this, and we were not going to just stop at some cheap restaurant to grab a bite. I had just bought expensive tickets to a play, and he could take me to a very nice dinner. I made reservations.

We arrived at the City Grill, and I asked to be seated in Janet's section. My son had dated Janet, and I'd always liked her. We had stayed friends. She and I started talking, and my romantic dinner was gone. But it was nice to see her and be there with Steve, and the view from our window seat was terrific.

Then we went to the play. He kept kissing me on the neck and making out with me while people were all around us. Where was my no, that does not work for me? It was embarrassing to me. But it was Steve, and he cared. Isn't that how you see it?

We left and went back to my place, as he had picked me up. We wasted no time and went straight to bed. He kept saying that he had to get home soon. His kids were there, and he needed to be there in an hour or two. But we had time for us of course. We got into bed, and we fit in every way. His dick was my perfect fit, and his lips on mine kissing me felt right. I was so gaga for him I could not stop looking at him and feeling so good inside; I would just stare at him in desire. I wanted to keep him and spend more time with him. I finally had someone who I loved to feel and look at and be with. And yes, he made very good money, so he could afford me. I had finally made it. This was the guy for me.

We were lying there, and I just kept staring at his face as I lay there beside him, our naked bodies pressed together. I was on a high.

Then Steve spoke. He told me that us being together was so great and that he wanted this to continue. I was just melting. My naked body felt so good lying next to his naked body. And hearing his words was amazing.

Then the other ball dropped. He said that he felt that he had just started getting out and meeting women and he needed to meet a few more women. Then he would make his decision about who he wanted to be with. He wanted me to hang in and be there. Who knew? I could be the one.

As you know, my jaw dropped, and a coldness swept across me. I was naked, and I wanted my clothes on. I wanted to hide. I just looked up at him and said, "That does not work for me!"

He looked at me, stunned and a little shocked and said, "It doesn't?"

I said, "No, it doesn't."

He told me again that I could be the one. He just needed time to meet other women and make sure. He was actually saying that he wanted to do other women until he found the one he wanted to be with. Oh my God, what a letdown; what a hurt. I had gone gung ho like always, and look what I got—hurt.

Steve left, and I just cried and cried. I was so hurt and felt so dirty. I always hoped that, one time, a man was going to be real inside, not just a dog in heat sniffing for pussy.

Steve and I tried to get together a few times after that, but I just couldn't. He would text me every holiday to wish me happy holidays. I told him to stop, but he didn't.

Steve asked me a few times to get together, but I said no. I knew he just wanted sex. I would sometimes say, "Okay, but only for dinner, no dessert." So we would always figure a way out.

One time about a year later, we agreed to meet for just dinner. We set the date for 5:00 p.m. at Five Spice in Lake Oswego. He asked over and over if he could pick me, and I said no. He knew if he did, he had me. And he was right; I would not say no to him if we got that close to a bed. We were going to meet on Thursday, and on Sunday, he texted to ask me if we were still on for Thursday. I called back, and we started joking and having fun talking about our upcoming meeting. He asked again about picking me up, and I said no; we would meet and see how the evening went. It had been a while, and it would be good to have quality time together.

Monday came, and he texted me, "See you at five at Five Spice." The prospect of seeing Steve again and just talking made me happy. And who knew, maybe down the road …

Thursday morning came, and my phone beeped, indicating that a text message had come in. The message was from Steve. He said that I was going to be mad at him, but he could not make it tonight. He had just heard from his son that he had to go to a parent-teacher thing at school. His son had forgotten to tell him until that morning. Could we make it another time?

I had known he was going to cancel; after all, this would be dinner and no sex. He would not be picking me up, even though he had asked to do so four or five times. That was the first clue.

Who was I to want something more than just sex in my life? Was there even more? For the first time in my life, I was thinking of more. But why not just be with Steve? I believed that I was worth more than just sex, and I wanted more. I just didn't really know what yet. I was still on my learning path. I felt I was being guided. I did not know how big the change that was occurring in was at the time.

Steve still texted me on holidays. On New Year's Eve in 2009, I got a text from him wishing me happy New Year. I called him to wish him the same. He asked what I was doing for New Year's, and I told him I was staying in. He said he was too. And he did not have any kids; they were all staying at friends for the night. We talked a little bit, and then he said I should come over to his house and have a drink.

I thought, *Why not?* This was Steve. He had no one yet, and he was asking me to his house in Camas. I said maybe. I would think about it and let him know.

He called again later that day and suggested that we meet for a drink and a spot by his house and then go back to his house. How did that sound? It was sounding better. I just wasn't getting the feeling again like I'd had before.

Later that evening, he called and left a message. "Where are you? I thought we were meeting."

I had never said I would meet. I was just listening to him. I could not go. A girlfriend asked me why not? "It's Steve, and he wants you to go to his house on New Year's Eve?"

The invitation did not seem so impressive to me. Why hadn't he called a few days earlier or asked me to dinner? When it came down to it, it was still a call for sex, no matter what night it was.

After that, I asked him to please stop texting me. I did not care to hear from him. And that was that. I have no idea what happened to him.

I had met four guys in a year, and I'd only had sex with one of them. Only one guy had gotten to me, and he had hurt my soul, my heart.

BOB NUMBER TWO: THE ATTORNEY

I still had a profile on an online dating site, Plenty of Fish. I decided to meet with a man. He did not have the look I wanted, but he seemed nice and he was older.

Bob Number Two was very nice. An attorney for a firm in downtown Portland, he had money. He had two homes and enjoyed attending social events about town like I did. He was tall, six foot one, and slender. We met for a drink and laughed a lot and enjoyed some nice conversation.

We went to dinner, and that was nice. He was very much a gentleman. We kissed. At first I wasn't sure how this felt, though I thought it was good. Then we met again. He walked me to my door, and I asked him in. We made out, and this time, I did not like his kissing. He seemed to just go into a trance. His lips would be on mine, but he did nothing but rest his lips against mine. His thoughts were completely focused on his hard cock. He was into the feeling of being hard and forgot I was there. Before he left, he asked if I would like to get together again.

He called and said he wanted to make dinner for me. How nice. We planned on me staying the night so we would not have to watch the time and could just enjoy the evening. I made it clear that I did not want to have sex. We had just met, and I was not ready to go there. Did he hear me? I don't know, probably not.

He had a great, big, new home. It wasn't decorated how I would have decorated it, but it was nice. He made appetizers and wine and a great dinner. We sat in front of the fireplace and had a great evening.

When it was time for bed, we went to his bedroom, and that was fine He got into bed, and I went into the bathroom and got undressed. I kept my white lace bra and underwear on. As I walked to the bed, Bob pointed out the oil that was on his nightstand. He said it was to help get him started.

I reminded him what we had talked about. I was just going to sleep next to him, and we had agreed to no playing around.

"Oh, yes," he replied. "I remember, but just in case, this is here."

We lay close together and just slept; that was it.

The next morning, we had coffee and read the paper. It was one of those nice mornings with a nice man. The holidays were coming up. Even though we had just met a few weeks ago, Bob wanted me to meet his family and come to Thanksgiving dinner. His daughter was flying in the night before the holiday, and he was taking her and his new grandbaby out to pizza. Bob wanted me to go with them and meet her. I said no; it was too soon.

He called on Thanksgiving Day to make sure I was coming over for dessert to meet his family. What a compliment. But I wasn't that into him. This was too much for me. I did not go.

We went out a few more times, but eventually I told him that I didn't think we should go out anymore. I liked him and had fun with him. I just did not want to be that committed to anyone. I meant to him.

Later he called and asked why I wanted to end our budding romance. I told him I would be honest with him. For one thing, when he kissed me, he got a hard on and then he went into a trance and forgot I was there. It turned me off. We talked for two hours.

We stayed friends and went out to dinner a year later around the holidays and again the next year. I just wasn't into him. I really wanted to be his friend and liked going out with him and talking. He was so much fun and so real. We still talk now and then.

CHAPTER SEVENTEEN

SEXUAL HARASSMENT

IN JUNE 2009, I TOOK another job as an apartment manager and moved to the Terwilliger Terrace Apartments.

I was extremely happy to have this job. The apartment management company that had hired me seemed to be a very nice company.

DANA: SEXUALLY OBSESSED

One day, six weeks after I'd been hired, John, the owner of the management company, arranged for the owner of the building to meet me. On the appointed day, John arrived first, and then a knock sounded on the door.

Dana, the building owner came in, and I was pleasantly surprised. He was tall and half Asian. I was attracted to him right away. We started talking about my duties, and I found talking to Dana very interesting. He had a great amount of energy, and I could see that we were both attracted to each other.

I thought about Dana a lot. I had heard he was single, and I wanted to ask him out the next time he came into town. I had not dated anyone for a year now. I was kind of turned on thinking about him.

Six weeks later, Dana came into town. John said that his return so quickly was unusual. Normally, Dana only came to town two, maybe three, times a year.

The three of us walked the property, and then John left. I asked Dana if he was single. He said he had been separated for a year. "Why do you ask?" he pressed gently.

"I thought we could go to dinner," I said.

He liked the idea and said he would be back at 7:30. He arrived right on time, and we went to a nice restaurant in downtown Portland. We had a great time, laughing, talking and holding hands. This was great; a nice date was all I'd expected or wanted.

We got back to my place, and I don't know why, but I did what I always do. I asked if he wanted to come in and talk. Why couldn't I just leave things alone?

We went in, and the next thing I knew, Dana was running down the stairs to my bedroom. I stood at the top of the stairs in amazement. What just happened?

I went down to my bedroom, and there he was in my bed and ready. His body was very white, and his nice, long, hard cock was brown. I thought, *I guess this is okay*. I hadn't expected this at all.

I got into bed, and oh my God, he turned me every way but loose. He was great in bed. He had a nice-size cock—the perfect fit. Orally, he made me nuts for hours; he just would not stop. When he went inside of me to fuck me, I just about had an orgasm right then. We had so much fun. He was wild.

Three or four hours later, he left. I wasn't sure about what had just happened. As good as he'd felt, something was wrong.

Dana came back to town four weeks later and planned on staying the night with me. I said, "Oh, okay."

After getting a bite to eat, we came back to my place and showered. And he turned me every way but loose again. He knew how to take care of a woman sexually. His mouth was wonderful and then his cock went in, and I thought I'd left the world; nothing else mattered but this feeling.

Afterward, we lay there actually talking. That was nice too. He was kind and loving and trying to be thoughtful.

Then the words that I had wondered about in the back of my mind came. Dana said that he did not want me to get hurt, adding that, of course I had known what I was getting into.

I thought, *No*, but just listened.

Dana explained that, after all this time, he was thinking about reconciling with his wife.

I asked when he planned to do this, and he said in a few months, well soon.

"That is good," I said. And then I pressed for more details. "Have you set a date? How soon is soon?"

When Dana just said, "Yes," I knew I had to press further.

"Did this already happen?" I asked.

He simply said, "Yes."

I was shocked and devastated. I would not have let this happen if I had known that he was married and actually living with his wife. I would not do that to another woman. I couldn't help but wonder whether he had ever actually been separated from his wife, whether that had just been a lie. I told him that if I had known, I would not have gone to bed with him. I felt lied to and misled.

This was in September, and I did not hear from Dana for three months. That was good. I had been very worried about what would come of the situation.

On December 31, he called. I didn't answer. Then he called me five or six more times that day. I finally answered the phone, and he was so happy. We talked for a while. When we hung up, he said he wanted me to call him later. I didn't, and he called again.

The next week, Dana started calling again a lot. He said he wanted to send an air mattress up so that he could stay in one of the empty apartments. Sure he did. I figured that he had been a good boy for three months, and now he wanted to start this sex thing all over again. The air mattress scenario was likely his way of saying he wanted to stay with me.

It was not going to happen. I called John and told him what Dana wanted to do. I would probably have the apartment rented soon anyway. And if Dana was here, I would go nuts. He was very eccentric and high-strung; he was loud and demanding. Basically, he threw his weight around as the owner of the building. I explained that I just shrugged this behavior off and told Dana that, if he was going to talk that way, I would go outside until he was done. John told Dana that it was not a good idea for him to stay in the empty apartment.

I knew what was about to happen, and I did not want to go there with Dana. He was married. He just wanted me because he lived in California and I was convenient. Yes, the sex was great.

But Dana was obsessed with getting together with me again. He just could not leave it alone. He was calling all the time.

I sent an e-mail and told him that he needed to be happy where he was—with his wife—and that the situation did not work for me. I did lie and say that I had a boyfriend and was very happy with him. I wished Dana well and added that I wanted to keep our business arrangement intact and that was all.

Dana e-mailed back. He said he understood and what I had suggested would be fine. We would work together on his property, and our relationship would remain totally professional, nothing more.

I wish that was true. His e-mail sounded good. But Dana was utterly obsessed with having sex with me again. It was all he could think about. He started to come to the apartment complex often, saying he wanted to talk. He would be aggressive and make sexual comments in front of workers. It did not matter to him that I said, "No, no, no. Your situation does not work for me."

He would attempt to leave the apartment and come back five times to hug me. I never gave him reason to think there would be anything between us other than business.

John would come with Dana, and I would always ask him to stay until Dana left. "Do not leave me alone with him," I would beg.

Since Dana was so eccentric and high-strung, John could not wait to leave. He always had an appointment or some excuse to leave. Dana never wanted to leave. He and John would get to the complex at 11:00 a.m., and John would leave at noon. Dana would still be there at 7:30 in the evening. I would ask him to leave. I would be so tired, trying just to keep things professional. No one should be put in this position.

In March, Dana was coming to town again. We all prepared ourselves to deal with his high energy—a nice way of putting it. I was always left to take care of myself with Dana. John did not want to hear about what was going on with Dana or deal with the situation. As long as he did not have to have any more interaction than was absolutely necessary with Dana, he was happy. It wasn't fair.

But who said life was fair? I liked my job and enjoyed my tenants. Still, I was getting worn down and sinking into depression. I did not like always being on the defensive and struggling to keep things grounded. I was trying to say, "Just leave me the fuck alone," but Dana was the owner of the building I manage. Jobs didn't come around every day. It had taken me a year to find this one.

John and Dana came to check the property out and go over the finances. This time, they both left, which was a first. Shortly thereafter, the phone started to ring. It was Dana. I did not answer. I knew what he wanted. I wished he would go away. How many times does a person have to say no? He kept calling, and finally, I answered. He wanted to take me to dinner. I said no. He insisted and insisted, trying to convince me by saying that I had to eat. On the tenth call, I said, "Okay."

He wanted to pick me up, but I said no. I would meet him across the street at the Mexican restaurant that I frequently went to by myself.

We sat in a booth, and he slid in beside me. We ordered a drink and something to eat. Then—was he crazy?—he got his dick out under a napkin and grabbed my hand in an attempt to place it on his cock.

I just said, "Put that thing away. I don't want it."

When he got up to go to the bathroom, the waitress came over and asked if I was okay. I wasn't, but I said I was. The waitress had seen me often, as I came to the restaurant regularly just to have an appetizer and a drink. I don't cook, and this place was across the street.

Dana came back and started again. We finished eating and left the restaurant. I was so tired of just saying no. Outside, he shoved me against the brick wall. He took his dick out again, wanting me to go down on him. We were between two open restaurants—the one we'd just left and a pizza place. People were coming out of both. It was dark but well lit enough that someone could see what we were doing. He turned around and leaned on the wall and pulled me tight up against him, pushing my hand onto his cock.

I was sick. This was enough! I just went and got into my car. He wanted to come home with me.

"No," I told him. "It is not going to happen."

I got home, and a half hour later, he called. He told me that he loved me and that he would call me tomorrow. Dana did call me in the morning. He said that maybe he had spoken too soon.

I just said, "Well, you got caught up in the moment. Sometimes one says things like that."

The sexual harassment never stopped.

I called an attorney friend and asked him what he thought about my situation. He said that sexual harassment wasn't his area of expertise, so he gave me the name of an attorney who handled matters like mine.

I called, and while the attorney was kind enough to talk with me right away, he chewed me out. "When are girls and women going to learn that, once you say no, you never go out with them again?" he lamented. He explained that accepting another date takes away the no, making the man feel that it's okay to start up again, as if the situation had never stopped.

The attorney said that I did not work for the owner; I worked for the management company. He said that I needed to talk to someone at the company, which was supposed to protect me and handle the situation in a way that would keep me from losing my job.

Dana just fired John, along with the company that I was working for. He hired a new management company and told the company that I was to stay on managing the apartment complex.

I decided to follow the attorney's advice and talk to my new employers, a company called The Management Group located in Vancouver, Washington, about what was going on. The Management Group was made up of women, and I thought, *All right. This could work.*

I talked to Loya, the new company's portfolio manager and the person who overlooked my work on the property on Dana's behalf. What a mistake. In the end, this company and its employees harassed me for six months.

I had told Loya everything I was dealing with from Dana. I showed her the e-mails he'd sent me and told her about all the sexual advances he made. I explained that I was at my wit's end and utterly tired of saying no and of having to watch every move I made around him. She said the company would make sure I would not have to deal with Dana again. This backfired. At first, as I was learning the new company's ways of doing things, the people I worked with had been very nice. Then they started to be rude, and the help I needed to learn their program wasn't there. The company higher-ups started to warn me that they would write me up if I didn't get things in on time. *Wait,* I thought, *I have not been taught yet how this company wants thing done*. How could I do what they wanted? They need to show me how first. Instead, they had something to say about everything I did. They put me on warnings in regard to their rules. I think they set me up on occasion. I soon realized that telling Loya and the others about Dana and asking them to protect me was not working. Dana was the owner of the building and the source of the company's money. I was just a worker, the manager of the building. I knew I should not have said anything. I should have dealt with the Dana situation myself. I went into an even deeper depression. I needed to quit.

I e-mailed Dana and said that I had told the company everything. In January 2010, I lost my job. It was the best thing that could have happened to me.

Dana called in January and asked, "Where is my Marilyn?" He wanted to meet with me. He was still obsessed with the great sex we'd had; his nice cock could not forget me. This was not good. I'd spent a terrible year of my life trying to make someone understand the word *no*.

CHAPTER EIGHTEEN

CLEANSING OF MY SOUL
IN WILSONVILLE

Moving to Wilsonville, Oregon, was a great decision. I loved it there; it was place where I could make a new start. I would end up living in Wilsonville for almost a year. By then, I hadn't dated for three and a half years. During that time, I'd had sex maybe six times with two men. I was walking and writing my book and really enjoying myself. I was making plans and setting goals.

A few months after I moved into my new place, I felt very balanced. My life was filled with a sense of completeness. Over all, I felt calm and well rounded.

Then suddenly, I started feeling sick. My body hurt, and everything I ate went straight through me. I was getting mad at everything. Someone would look at me wrong, and I'd want to punch the person in the nose. I would think thoughts like this and worse.

This wasn't me. I liked people. Why was I hating everyone around me and wanting to thrash out and hurt someone? Who was I and what was happening to me? I felt like a mean, hateful person. I found myself fantasizing about breaking someone's legs. I hated life. I hated people. I felt rage and the desire to hurt. I just hated everything. I was filled with extreme anger, and I wanted revenge. I had never felt hate before, had never wanted to hurt others.

This went on for a month or two. Everything I ate would make me sick, even simple things like rice. What was going on? I had always loved people and been very social. I had wanted to help everyone. But not now. I couldn't figure out who I was or what had happened to me or why I was feeling this way. It was very scary. I had never experienced anything like this before.

One morning, I woke up and felt calm, like life was very good. I felt balanced—a different feeling than I'd ever had. I felt cleansed. It was as if, during the last few months, I had experienced all the hurt and anger that I'd kept inside—at my dad for being an alcoholic and my mom for putting me down, at my ex who had beat me, at all the dating that had gone badly, at the way my kids had treated me hurtfully. All that I had held inside that I could not talk to anyone about, telling myself I just needed to be bigger than the hurt, to hold it in and move on, had moved through me.

This was strange. I had gone through a cleansing that had washed away all the hurt and pain I had ever felt. That pain had completely taken over my body and had made me mean and angry and wanting to thrash out. All that hurt had made me sick to my stomach, and I had hated everything. And now I had been released from my hidden thoughts of hurt. I felt total forgiveness. It was such a great feeling. And just as I had wondered who I was during the sickness, I wondered again, now who am I? I felt so strange, like a totally new person.

I was ready to live life to the fullest, learning how to be this new person. How had this happened? How had I been cleansed and healed?

Along my path of learning and growing and trying to be the best I can be, I have read many books. I read self-help books from authors such as John Gray and Deepak Chopra, along with many titles from Oprah's list. I attended seminars with great speakers. I believe that, after twenty years of self-help and opening myself up to living, loving, and being the best me, I had come to understand the dysfunction from my childhood and move past my early years of life. As you know, I had lived life from the outside of my chest; I did not feel inside. I had thought I could find my life through sex—that sex was the only way to feel. I had lived for just those moments of sex; everything else felt empty.

I had given up. I had no goals and no desires. Without these things, we are empty and lost—just living day to day. Now I was waking up thinking about life and what I really wanted.

You never know where life will take you. I'd had a good life. I'd traveled, lived in million-dollar homes, and vacationed on yachts. I had lived many different lives and had experienced so many men. I had visited places all over the world. I had lived an extremely wealthy lifestyle more than once. I had lived in poor, well average, circumstances. And all of these things had been, in the end, good things to have experienced.

Now what should I desire? I couldn't just sit around with nothing to desire and no goals to work on. Everyone should always have a dream, a goal, and things to cross off a bucket list. Dreaming keeps our minds busy.

What did I want in life that I had not yet had? I had spent the past year wondering what I needed now. I had done so much. What else could I want to experience?

And then it dawned on me. Despite the two hundred or so men I'd had in my bed, I had never been in love. This was what I wanted next in my life!

How would I go about finding love? I didn't date. I didn't want to go out to the bars again; that never worked.

I was just putting my desire out there to the universe.

I went to a tarot card reader, mainly to ask about my book. To my shock and surprise, the reader told me that I would be in love. What? I thought. No way. I told him that I could not go there. "I do not date and haven't in almost four years," I explained, adding, "That has never happened."

The tarot reader assured me that it was going to happen no matter what I did. I did not go out or date. How could this happen? I let the subject go. I just wanted to know about my book. I could not imagine that what he was saying could ever be real.

The summer had come to an end. It was September now, and I needed to go out, get involved with people, and start mingling. I wasn't ready to date. But I did want to meet someone and be in love.

One night, I decided to go out and meet my girlfriends. I took a deep breath and made myself get dressed. It took everything I had to bring myself to go out.

I put on a new dress, and it felt great. I wasn't sure about this, but I was going to wear my dress. I was headed to downtown Portland to meet my girlfriends. As I was driving, I just turned off the freeway and headed to The Lake House in Lake Oswego, one of my favorite places. It was right on the lake and had a bar outside. I had not been there all summer; I had been avoiding getting out in the scene again.

I did think I was done with my book and men! To my surprise, I found one more to end my book with.

CHAPTER NINETEEN

A NIGHT THAT WOULD CHANGE MY LIFE FOREVER

JOHN NUMBER THREE: THE CHARMER

I HAD MADE MYSELF GO OUT. Something kept pulling me to go, as if I had no choice.

I walked into the outside bar overlooking the lake. I immediately saw a social friend who I'd known for years standing at the bar. Gary, who was a good-looking man, waved to say hi, and I walked over to him. He greeted me very warmly and then pointed to a man sitting next to him at the bar. He introduced me to the man, whose name was John. As soon as I looked at him, I raised my eyebrows. I thought to myself, *I could date this man.*

John asked me to sit and visit. Gary got up and said, "Take my chair." He was going to talk with other friends.

I sat down and John and I started talking. He was funny, good-looking, and a little naughty. He said his jaw had dropped when I walked in. He thought I was his ex-girlfriend for a moment. I looked just like her. John looked at me and said I could be someone he could date.

He seemed to do well for himself, which is something I preferred in a man. He gave me his card, and I saw that he was a senior project manager for a big company. That meant he could afford me and the things I liked to do. He liked the slit in my dress and put his fingers on my knee, teasing the slit. My dress was low, and he found it to be nice and pleasing to look at. He was very complimentary He apologized for being a little tipsy. That impressed me. I had a lot of fun talking to him.

John asked me out for the next night, which was Saturday. He said he wanted to take me to dinner. He wanted me to see who he really was when he wasn't as drunk as he felt he was. He said that was not him. He kept apologizing.

I said yes. He gave me his card and asked me to call him in the morning. John seemed to really want to show me the real him.

I called the next morning, and he was happy to hear from me. He said he wasn't sure if I would call, but he had been waiting and hoping for the call. We made plans to meet downtown at the Paragon.

I got there first. He walked in. At six foot one, he was tall and dressed in a nice white shirt and black pants—my favorite. We had a drink and then walked over to a nice restaurant for dinner. He didn't seem as into me as he had the night before. John drank wine that night; he said it kept him straight. He had been drinking whisky on Friday night. We had a nice date, and when he walked me to my car, he asked me out again and said he would call. I thought a hug or a kiss would have been nice. But it did not happen. I figured he just wasn't that into me. He was so different than he'd been the night before. Oh well, we'd had a nice date anyway.

A few days later, John called and asked if I would like to meet for a drink. I figured, *Why not?*

What a change. He was now acting like he had the first night. John was drinking Maker's Mark. Apparently, whisky helped him let go. He was fun to talk to and be with.

We started meeting on Fridays for happy hour and getting together one night during the week. In the second week, we spent the night together. Wow, he was huge; it hurt so good. I loved looking at him and just being with him.

Soon we were spending every Friday and Saturday night together. John told me everything I wanted to hear. He was unbelievable. I started feeling like I was thirty years old, and I was happy just to be around him. I felt beautiful, young, and full of energy. We always met for happy hour on Friday nights when he got off work. He drank a lot and would get drunk. But I liked him so much. Everything he said made me want him more. He was perfect.

John was not into kissing, but we had great sex. It wasn't the best sex I'd ever had, but I felt the best feeling in bed with him that I'd ever had. I had not had an orgasm with a man for five years. Now, when John slid his giant, well-oiled cock inside me, I would feel a sensation that was overwhelming. I had never felt it before. I realized he was hitting my G-spot. I hadn't known where it was before.

John would complain that I wasn't having a clitoral orgasm. I didn't care. I was so happy that, when he went inside me, I just felt this sensation all over my body. I loved his look and his great body. He did have some loose skin on his tummy, but he was yummy. I couldn't have cared less about having more. John was so good looking to me. He was tall, and I loved his broad shoulders. When he smiled at me, my clothes just fell off. His voice was deep and strong. This good-looking man made very good money and had once been a millionaire. He had a high-end job and was doing great again. He wanted me, and I felt like a young woman.

If I had a list of everything I wanted in a man, John was it. Every time he said anything, I melted. I told him I was keeping him. If he was who he said he was, he was everything I had wanted in a man. I hurt for him every night when he was not with me. We would text each other; we could not sleep for missing each other.

As soon as John had one drink, I could feel him start to change. He would become extremely sexy and happy. By the time he'd had four, he was wonderful. He would compliment me and become completely romantic and caring. He told me he just drank on Fridays and the weekends to unwind from the week of pressure at work. He never drank during the week.

Four weeks into our dating, we went back to the Lake House. The Lake House was closing for good, and the establishment was throwing itself a good-bye party.

We walked in, and John started to bounce around and introduce me to his co-workers. He said, "This is the love of my life. You will be seeing a lot of her." I just stood tall and so happy to be seen with him.

A younger lady kept coming up to him, but he never introduced me to her. At one point, he was gone, and I saw that he was talking to her. I wanted to leave. I did not like this behavior. It was almost as if I was not there.

Jeff, one of John's friends from work, asked me what was wrong. I told him that John was off talking to another woman and that I wanted to leave. Jeff said that John had just had too much to drink and that he was trying to wind down from the stress at work. He told me to just go over and get him.

So I did. I went over and took his hand and pulled him away from the young woman and back to his friends from work. I thanked Jeff.

Soon, John was standing against the wall, and I asked what was going on. "Are you okay?"

I just about lost it when I heard his answer. "Marilyn, I am just telling you what you want to hear." Flag—*big, red* flag.

I have never forgotten those words.

Not knowing what else to do, I told him that I wasn't listening to him right then. He'd had a lot to drink, and I figured it was just the alcohol talking.

I would later learn that what he'd said was absolutely true. I should have listened to those words and walked out right then. It would have saved me five and a half months of hell.

We do have things we ignore—things someone says that don't make sense and actions we question. Stuff like that with John started to add up, but I let my feelings and his look take over. I believed he had to mean most of what he said. No one would say all the things they are and not be any of them, right?

I drove home. We had left his car at my place.

We always had lots of sexual play on Friday and Saturday nights. I thought that he was so lucky to be able to get a hard on. Little did I know, he used Viagra. But what his cock did to me! When he was on the bed on his back, I would move to get on top of him. His dick was hard, and I would oil him stroking his cock. He was so big. Yum. I would have to raise my leg up high to straddle him and slide down on his cock. His cock always hit my G-spot, and I would have an orgasm. Such a sensation!

I had always wanted a good-looking guy, and now I had one who was everything on my list of what I wanted in a man. This was too good to be true.

Was I paying attention to any signs, to any of the red flags? No.

John and I were telling each other that we loved one another. I got so obsessed with this feeling that I had never felt before. I felt beautiful and young and full of energy. John brought me back to life. I wanted sex again; the desire was back, and it was strong and filled with passion. We had sex three to five times every weekend until I moved in with him.

On Halloween night, we attended a big party in downtown Portland, the Erotica Ball. John dressed in leathers chaps, and he drank a lot. I put on a lace, crotchless bodysuit; a short, black skirt; a leather vest that showed off my breasts; and boots. I felt hot. We had fun. John did try to move a little on the dance floor. We left before it got real naughty.

This was a night to remember. John and I got into the shower, and he was at his naughtiest; what fun. He played with me all over, and I played with him. We got into bed, and he got a camera out. I normally would not like this, but he positioned me every nasty and naughty way we could think of—bent over, with my legs in the air and spread apart. I felt myself while he licked me, and I enjoyed.

I looked at the pictures, and I must say I was happy. I looked good, not my age. Thank heavens.

When he got into bed, we had great sex every way but loose. What a night!

John kept asking why I wasn't with him every night. And I agreed; I wanted to be with him every night. We would text each other at 4:00 a.m. saying that we couldn't sleep. I would text him that I was backing up across the bed where he was supposed to be. "I need you," I would tell him. After a night of drinking, he would wake up at 4:00 a.m. with a hard on. I had never been a real morning person; my main high is in the evening or afternoon. But I got to the point that I was waking up at four every morning even when John wasn't. That was all we talked about then.

He fed me everything I needed to hear. I thought I had seen everything and was very intuitive. Much later, I would think of a well-known phrase—too good to be true. If you ever find yourself in a situation where you're thinking of this phrase, you should check things out closer. After all, this is your life.

I just went with my feelings. I gave up everything and went for it with John! He had to be who he said he was, right?

I was in love, very much in love. This man had made me fall for him in a way that I had never fallen for anyone before. I had loved, but I had never been in love! Wow, I had found just what I'd asked for; I had the only thing in my life I had not experienced—being in love. Everything I wanted in a partner John said he wanted too.

Oh my God, I thought, let's not wait to get this started. Finally, I said okay, let's move in together. We found a place. John moved in with nothing but his clothes, a TV, and a mat to sleep on.

I gave my notice and packed up. A few months later, I moved in. I left the security of my nice place, where I had written my book and gotten into shape and learned to love life. This was the place where I had been so happy to be dating John and sleeping with him, to know that he was my man. Here, I had heard the unbelievable things he would say to me.

The day I moved in, I felt something was wrong. The move was not as exciting as it should have been. We did not drink a bottle of champagne to celebrate us being a real couple. John did not seem like John. He asked me to give him time, saying that he would come around and adjust to living together. That night, I wanted to go home. I cried. I did not want to be there. John did not give me a warm, happy feeling. It just got worse and worse.

John turned cold the day I moved in. It was the beginning of the five months of hell. Sex slowed down almost to nothing. How could someone be so different from the person he had said he was? I could not understand this. We'd had two and a half months of fun, drinking, and junk food. I realized that it was about the alcohol; when he was drinking, we were having fun.

John was not the man I believed him to be; he just told me everything I wanted to hear. But now that we were living together, the lies started to add up, and the sex seemed to fade away. John kept saying that his job was to blame; he was under too much stress. He asked me to be patient.

The number one lie had to do with alcohol; he drank every night, not just on weekends. Where had I been? Certainly not listening to my inner voice. John was definitely an alcoholic. The first night I met him was who he was; he wasn't the man from our first date, when he had been putting on a show—see, I can be sober and boring.

I still adored my good-looking man and wanted us to be a real couple. I asked him to try and make it work.

I put our place together, trying to make a home for us. It was December, and I wanted a Christmas tree. I wanted a real Christmas with my man and family and friends. Notice that I am saying *I* a lot.

There were so many things I didn't understand. John slept on the couch a lot. I had not yet met his kids or seen the place he'd lived in before our place. He was cold and wouldn't say hi when he came home from work. He'd just go to the bathroom and look in the mirror. Then he'd lie on the couch, as if I wasn't even there.

I bought presents and put them under the tree. I couldn't wait to share this special time with John. I imagined us doing festive things together.

The day before Christmas Eve came, and he had only shopped for his kids. He'd gotten one present that I thought was for us. We'd looked at this special coffeemaker at several places, and he had thought it would be nice for us to have one so we could share coffee in the mornings. I thought it was a neat idea.

That night, we met a special friend of mine, Peter. I really wanted Peter to meet the man I was now living with, my partner. I wanted to start getting out with my partner and enjoying life with my man, like I had never done before.

Peter was living with Pam, and the two of them joined us. Pam was very nice. I enjoyed meeting her and having all of us get together.

At one point Pam said to John, "You are a hard-core drinker."

"Why do you say that?" John replied.

"Well," she said, "you are drinking whiskey, and doubles at that. And that is your fifth drink."

I was so blinded. I just wanted to take care of him.

That night, he had twenty drinks. He was totaled. I did not care. I just took him home and tucked him in bed. All Christmas Eve day, he stayed in bed or on the couch. He never went out to buy me a present. I was getting hurt.

We did not plan any family things, something he'd said he liked and wanted to do together when we first met. We only drank together. We ate junk food, not good food. We didn't take walks in the evening or work out together, things he couldn't wait to start doing as soon as we move in together. Nothing that he said was happening. All I saw was a cold and drunken John.

Christmas was here. John got out of bed, and we wrapped his kids' gifts, or rather, I did. Then he had me wrap the coffeemaker as a gift for his ex-wife. Something was very wrong with this picture. Hmm—ex-wife or not? I often wondered whether John was still married. I asked him many times. He would just say, "Why do you ask?"

I would explain that I just felt "it"—that something was wrong.

He would want to know what it was that I felt.

I should have run then. It didn't matter where I went; I should have just gotten out.

John didn't want to open my gifts to him, and he did not get me a gift. I did not understand anything at this point. Who was this man I was living with? He was not the passionate man I had met, the caring person who had told me what I'd wanted to hear. This was not the man who had made me laugh and with whom I'd been so happy!

Every Saturday and Sunday morning, we would have coffee together and talk. He would talk to me. He would acknowledge me and make me feel cared about, make me believe that I meant something to someone. How could I not have seen all this coming? This did not make sense.

I went to see my kids, and John went to see his. I was sitting with my son, and out of the blue, my son said that he knew what was going on.

"What?" I asked. I had not said anything to my kids about how John had been and how badly he'd been treating me since I'd moved in. I started crying, and I just wanted to die. I was so unhappy and hurt.

Before I'd left to see my kids, John had said that we would go out and have a nice dinner. That was not his thing. I knew he'd back out. He never followed through with what he said. I called, and he was at home.

"What?" I said. "How long have you been there?"

He answered simply, "Awhile." He said he could not find a place open, so we might just have to go to a fast food place.

That was not going to work for me. While I drove, I called some very nice restaurants. I found one open. I knew John would be shocked.

When I got home, I put him on the spot. He could not back out. We went to City Grill. It was fun. He was like the man he'd been on our first date, reserved.

He opened his presents when we got home and thought nothing of not having a present for me. I had spent eighty dollars on alcohol for Christmas Eve—a bottle of Baileys and Grand Marnier for me and a bottle of Maker's Mark, John's whisky that he said he only drank on Fridays and weekends. I gave him the receipt and said he owed me that money! I made him pay for it, the lazy fucker.

John had the week off, and we'd planned to go to Sun Valley on Wednesday evening. The day started out badly and was a complete mess; he changed everything we'd planned. He didn't take his shirts to the cleaners and said he was going out but would be back. He wanted me to meet him at the airport. I told him no, that we would keep the plans the way we'd arranged. He started laundry a few hours before we were to leave for the airport.

We got on the plane and had a great flight. We landed, and the evening turned out to be a good one. John met one of his friends, and we all had dinner the next day together. It was fun.

Then all hell broke loose. Out came the real John—the guy drank every day and, as it turned out, needed prescription drugs too. He stayed drunk the entire time we were in Sun Valley and finished a whole bottle of prescription drugs, ninety tablets, that I'd given him four weeks earlier. I went to get one so I could sleep, and they were gone. This drunken lowlife was not looking good. I would catch him in the bar drinking in the afternoon. I just wanted to go home.

One night, we went to town, and he, of course, ordered his Maker's Mark. Once he had his drink, he turned his back on me. I felt all alone again. I walked through the place talking to people. He did not even know I had walked away.

I met a man and enjoyed talking to him. He asked whether I was alone, and I answered, "Kind of. I'm with a guy who doesn't even know I'm here."

John came up to me and said he wanted to leave. He told me to just give him the keys, saying that I should stay and have fun.

What? No way was I staying somewhere I didn't know.

As we walked down the street, John kept sliding and slipping on the ice. He just wanted to argue. He wanted me to give him the keys. I said I would once we were in the car but not before. He grabbed my arm and pulled me to him.

I looked at him and said, "You ever do that again and you'll be going to jail."

When we got back to the hotel, he went to the room to pass out. I did not want to be with him, so most of the time while we were there, I stayed out in the hall and read or slept.

John spent New Year's Eve day drunk. The staff at Sun Valley Lodge knew me as the woman who walked the halls by herself. I sat in the bar on New Year's Eve by myself crying and calling my daughter. I felt lost.

The front desk guy, Larry, tried to help me. I just wanted to go home and leave this horrible man who thought that everything was all about him. I had met the bus driver from the lodge and had made arrangements to have him come back to pick me up in the morning. Earlier, I had gone to the room and taken my plane ticket out of

John's briefcase. He was passed out. He was embarrassing, ugly, and drunk; half the time, he couldn't even walk. The bus driver came back and talked with me on New Year's Eve. So we cheered together and had a small kiss at midnight.

The next morning, I got up early. John got up, and of course, he didn't even see what he had been doing. He said, "Just stay. What is wrong with you?"

When I got on the bus, John was leaning on the building wall looking sad, as if he had just lost his best friend. I was so happy to be leaving. I loved the holidays, and this had been the worst holiday season in my life.

Rather than the dream John had promised me, he'd given me a nightmare from hell. Ever since I had started living with him, our lives had been all about him and what he wanted. Was I nuts? Was I blind? What part of this did I not get? I had never put up with much in my life. If a situation wasn't good or was full of negativity, I just left and end it.

Where was the John I had first met—the man who was so perfect? Yes, if something seems too good to be true, then it is too good to be true.

But I was not done yet. I got home on January 1, 2012, feeling terribly hurt and confused. A few days went by, and I wondered what John was doing. He should have gotten home on January 2. I started missing him. Now who needed help?

We know he was sick, but I wanted to see him; I missed him. I got an e-mail from him in which he tried to explain his actions and said that he was missing me. He said that he was shocked by my behavior—that I had insisted on leaving and was running away. John said he thought that we were together for better or for worse and promised me that he would come around.

What was wrong with me? I just wanted him so badly that I texted him. And he wanted to meet too.

On January 5, a Thursday, we met at the Roadhouse. As I walked in, I saw him sitting at the bar, and I just wanted him. I took in his tall, strong features, his full head of hair, his white teeth, the jeans that fitted firmly around his tight ass, and his nice, big thighs.

We both wanted to make our relationship work. He said he had stopped drinking the hard stuff the day I left, that it made him crazy. He couldn't just have one or two without having ten or more. He swore that he was smart and could do this for us.

He did, but now who was he? He was reserved without alcohol. Drinking beer or wine, he just wasn't the man I met. But something more happened. He became mean and then angry and then full of rage. He grew cold and quiet. He no longer talked sweetly to me at all. We had sex less and less often. What was happening? He was rude and talked down to me. He told me to do my thing and not to count on him. "Why are you looking to me for anything?" he would demand.

He would tell me one day that he loved me and then say the next day that we should part. Once or twice a week, I would see the John I wanted. For a few hours, he would be caring and loving. I took those moments and thought, *Yes, we are together.*

The next day, he would be cold again, and the mean, angry John would be all I'd see for a week or two. One time, he did not acknowledge me for two weeks.

This wasn't working for me.

At one point, he had to go to Los Angeles. He asked me to go and said that, if I paid for the ticket, he would pay me back. I said no. I did not go. He left on a Wednesday morning, and we had sex. Well, I gave him a blow job to take care of my man. I asked him to call me every night, and he said he would of course.

That night he texted me a cold text, only after I had texted him. On Thursday, I checked out the medicine cabinet and realized that one of the two Viagra pills that had been there the night before he left was missing. Now there were two pills, but only one was a Viagra; one pill was oval-shaped, and the other was round. I cried all night. I was so hurt again; it just didn't end.

I e-mailed him on Friday, noting that something was missing from the medicine cabinet. I received no response. I did not hear from him the entire five days that he was gone.

Sunday night came, and he was due home at 10:00 p.m. I waited; no John. At 2:00 a.m., I started calling and texting, asking if he was okay.

What was going on? Had he taken someone with him? Had he planned to meet up with someone?

I couldn't make heads or tails from his behavior. Why was I still here trying to figure it out?

Finally I called, texted, and e-mailed him, leaving messages that I would be at his place of work at 9:00 am. I knew this would get his attention. It did. He called at 8:00 am and said not to come to his workplace. We would talk that night.

"Do you want to end us?" I asked.

He said he did, as that would be better for me.

"Don't always say what would be better for me," I replied. "Tell me what you want."

He said he wanted to part.

"Good," I said. "Now we will talk tonight." He needed to say it to my face.

It was a long day. When 5:30 came, he was not home. At 5:50, he walked in as if nothing was wrong. He just said, "Let's let it be and just move on."

Nope; we were going to talk.

John flat-out said that he wanted to end our relationship. This just wasn't what he wanted. He just did not have it to give and was not good at it anyway.

I said, "Great." I told him that I couldn't just move out. I needed to have a plan. (What, I wasn't planning my move already? I needed help.) Starting over would take me a few months. I was happy that we'd made way on what we need to do.

John lay on the couch as if he planned to sleep there. I told him that we could share the apartment. He said he could move and give me space. I didn't care what he did. He could stay, and I would do my own thing. We need not be enemies.

We talked it out to the detail, and he offered to pay for an apartment for me and help me out for a few months, since he had gotten me into this.

I got up to go to bed. I had a lot on my mind. I needed to make plans to move. As I left the living room, I heard a soft voice. "Can I come to bed with you?"

I turned in shock. What was he saying? He had just ended our relationship—what little of a relationship we'd had, which had dwindled to virtually nothing. We just shared an apartment.

I looked at him for a while and then decided that I guessed we could sleep together until I moved out. He got off the couch and seemed happy to get into bed. And yes, he wanted sex. What? He had just told me to move out and the he did not want us. Now he wanted to have sex. It seemed like ending things with me turned him on. We had some hot fucking, and we had a good time. This was sick.

As we lay there afterward, I asked, "So does this mean we are okay and will work on our relationship?"

I could not believe his answer. He said, "Just leave it alone. Don't make something out of it." He asked if I was PMSing, acting like we hadn't just had the conversation we had.

We went back to our old pattern. John would push me away and be mean one night and then treat me nice the next night, as if everything was good between us. Of course, I would think it was, and then we'd have a night of good sex, fun drinking, and wild talk. The next day, John would be cold for a week or two again.

I hung on to the few hours he gave me every week or two. I cried every night and sunk into a deep depression. I couldn't believe I was allowing myself to be treated like this. I wanted the John he had told me he was to come out.

I spoiled him and tried to make him happy. I did all kinds of things for him. I was patient. I bought his junk food for him. He did not like nice dinners or a good breakfast. He just liked his peanut M&Ms with diet coke for breakfast. In the evenings, he liked pizzas from a cardboard box or snack crackers—all junk.

His mood swings were a result of him coming off the hard stuff— the whisky and the prescription drugs. He always wanted mine, and I'd give them to him. I know now that, when I didn't he'd go through withdrawals and, with them, the mood swings.

John did not see himself doing any of these things; he acted as if whatever he did was okay. At one point, I told him that I would not support his prescription drug habit.

During the previous month, John had moved in and out three times in a week. I just looked at him and asked what was happening. Toward the end, I got caught up in the drama.

So many hurtful things happened. The problem was that I could not just move. I was on a limited income, and jobs were not happening. Or maybe I was so involved with this unhealthy relationship that I could not leave; I had become addicted to it.

Never, with all the men I had been with, had I seen the type of behavior that I was seeing from John. I did not know or understand what was happening with him.

CODEPENDENCY

My daughter kept saying, "Mom, you are codependent."

I would argue that I wasn't.

"Yes, you are," she would insist. "You always have been."

I knew I had never been involved in something like this before.

One day, I looked up *codependent*; I wanted to find out what it meant. I got a rude awakening; as I read about a codependent person, I was reading about myself. That was me every day—the words I was reading described what I was doing and how I felt. Yes, in this relationship I was codependent.

But that hadn't been true before. When things with other men had gone badly, I had just made up my mind that what was happening wasn't healthy for me and ended the relationship. This time, I was locked in. I was addicted and obsessed with making John happy. I was constantly waiting for that minute or two that he would talk to me nicely, maybe have sex with me, and say the words I wanted to hear.

John grew even colder, and he acted like he was doing me a favor to so much as talk to me and let me see him. What an ego. He was so into himself.

Now I understood why I was still there. And as I read more material about codependency, I understood more. I came across the term *narcissism*. I read that a codependent woman sometimes can get caught up in a relationship with a narcissistic man. As I read on, I saw clearly that this was John—the material described his every move, his pattern. The narcissistic man, I read, was good-looking, made great money, had a position at work that made him responsible for many people under him, and was an alcoholic or prescription drug abuser. When you met a narcissist, he would tell you what you wanted to hear. The narcissist was so good-looking; you couldn't help but fall in love with him. Then once you made a commitment, such as moving in together, getting married, or having kids, he turned cold and became mean. But every couple of weeks, he would be nice just to keep you there at his beck and call. The narcissist was only about himself and could only love himself.

Wow, this was powerful; I had an answer, an explanation for the behavior that I had gotten caught up in. I guess this form of psychosis—narcissism—typically resulted from a bad childhood, and there was no cure. Many websites on the subject gave the same advice to women who were entangled with a narcissist—run. The relationship would never be healthy, and everything would always be about him. The sites advised that women in my situation should get help, as narcissists were difficult to break away from.

Even after reading all this, I hurt. I printed the material so that

John could read about what was going on with himself. Of course, he could care less about helping himself. He liked who he was and wanted to remain exactly the same person, never understanding what was happening with other people around him.

I printed many copies of the material and left them everywhere. I asked him once whether he was embarrassed by himself and the way he acted. He would act like what was going on just didn't happen. I saw three different men in him. I always felt he was still married. I never met his kids. So many things happened that I just couldn't figure out what was true.

I would find out later, after I had finally moved out, that he was still legally married. He lived two lives. He admitted being married but added that it was only on paper. What a hurt I felt. This only brought up more questions. I found out that he had bought her a $20,000 car. Why I did not get a Christmas gift or a birthday gift? We were living together!

A month before the lease to the apartment was up, John moved out one day and back in the next. He moved back and forth three times that week. He got his own apartment. I was extremely hurt, but I knew we were getting close to the end.

John would text me and say things like, "It doesn't have to be this way. Can't we find a way to stay close?"

One time, he called and said that, for the life of him, he could not figure out why we couldn't get along! One day, he called three times and left a nice message. He said he knew I was his woman and that I was meant for him. He had never been treated so well or spoiled so nicely. He had felt truly loved from the day he met me.

One week before this, he'd moved his few things out in a fit of rage. Now, he was acting like this had never happened. What a roller-coaster ride. I have to say again how deeply hurt I was to discover that he was married.

Love in My Future

I finally found a place and moved. It is great. I have my bad days. But John does not know where I live, and I do not call him. I know he thinks I am still there for him and that everything is okay. I think of his cock because he gave me a sensation I never had before with another man.

He gave me something that made me feel alive, made my body wake up in a real sense. I desired sex again. He woke up my mind too, and I realized that I do want to feel and have a real relationship. That desire was what I had been hiding from all these years.

All the bad stuff that happened between us was an awakening to what life has to offer—to what I could truly feel inside. My whole body felt alive!

I had felt what it was like to really being in love—well in love with being in love. I know that now. What a great feeling. Now I know I can be with someone. It took a man that was extremely unhealthy to jerk me around. But now I feel that I can move on and find what I really want in a relationship. I will not go three and a half without dating again.

With John, I was both the happiest I'd ever been and the most hurt I'd ever been!

Ours was a very draining relationship; it was hurtful and depressing. Still, I will never forget what I got out of the time John and I had together. John brought me to life; he helped me know what being in love means. He opened my heart up. He awakened my body, mind, and soul and brought me alive sexually. And I believe he opened me up so that I could truly know how to love someone and want to have a great relationship—in the future.

We all want to believe in a man's word. My biggest fault was not listening to my inner voice!

God's greatest gift is love.